Leaders, Groups, and Influence

Leaders, Groups, and Influence

E. P. HOLLANDER
State University of New York at Buffalo

New York   OXFORD UNIVERSITY PRESS   1964

To my parents

Preface

In the social psychology of the 1960's, many viewpoints compete for the key to social influence. Under diverse headings, and in distinctive ways, lines of activity are pursued which speak to the question of how one person's action is affected by others. To account for this, there are discrepancy hypotheses and cognitive dissonance, theories of interpersonal perception, and measures of social desirability, dogmatism, and conformity. But, whatever their emphasis, all bear upon this central phenomenon.

Leadership is one avenue by which to approach social influence. It, too, has its distinguishing attributes. Some years ago in studying emergent leadership through sociometric procedures, I became especially interested in the basis for the assessments made. Further research indicated that quite separable categories of source were involved and that respondents could readily differentiate among these. The results suggested that, within various group settings, a kind of implicit interpersonal assessment was at work in several dimensions, among which are: perceived competence, in the sense of moving the group toward a valued goal; perceived conformity, in terms of living up to applicable group expectancies; and characteristics perceived as valued for their own sake.

The next step was to consider how leaders can be greater "conformers" to group norms while also, in the nature of things, being greater "innovators." Clearly, leadership involves alterations of group norms as a mode of exercising influence within certain reaches of group practice. It seemed likely that this was a matter of sequence, and as one achieved a level of higher status there would be certain changes occurring in expectancies so as to make innovation tolerated as a signalizing feature of "arrival."

One of the implications of this further work was that "nonconformity" for one member of the group might not be "nonconformity" for another. A convenient way of expressing these relationships was to conceive of status in the terms of credit awarded in the perception of others. By developing the concept of "idiosyncrasy credit," it was possible to account for sources of input to emergent status as well as for the functional properties of such status. Thus, emergent leadership depends upon one person's perception of another's behavior and personal attributes in time; it permits greater acceptance of one's assertion of influence; and it alters social expectancies so as to permit innovative behavior to be displayed within certain reaches of the group's activity. Without necessarily following a linear, additive function, an individual may rise in status, that is, gain credits, as an outgrowth of the impressions he conveys through ongoing interaction in the categories previously noted. He may then use these credits to act more independently in terms of the exercise of influence, but whether he does so or not depends in a variety of ways upon his own motivational and perceptual states.

Relationships such as these reflect the intermingling of leadership and conformity within influence process. These are not only related, in some sense of dependence upon one another; they also have significant ramifications both in terms of mechanisms which produce them as well as those governing their effects. Moreover, these internal and external aspects derive from interpersonal perception occasioned by literal face-to-face interaction as well as by certain modes of "simulated interaction," as for example when individuals harbor attitudes of prejudice toward persons whom they have just encountered. It seems evident, too, that *time*, represented in the sequential patterning of interaction and attendant perceptual changes, is a variable of singular importance to an understanding of social influence, whether in terms of conformity, leadership, attitude change, or whatever. Indeed, one implication of this is found in the degree to which phenomena of social interaction produce independent-dependent variable relationships which are of a reciprocating variety. Hence, the effect of conformity behavior at one period of time, for example, may be quite relevant to others' expectation of, or tolerance for, nonconformity at another period of time. In the case of attitude change, analogous mechanisms may be at work in terms of how the "communication source" is viewed in the context of past experience. This speaks not only to the problem of credibility, but to visibility, in a figure-ground sense, as well.

In this book, papers representing this view of leadership are augmented by some new chapters which develop its structure. The essential theme of the volume is that leadership is one aspect of a broader influence process feeding into conformity, attitude change, interpersonal attraction, and so on. The first three chapters introduce this main theme in various forms.

Part Two presents four research papers, all of which grew out of studies in military settings, the first three involving naval aviation cadets during the Korean War. This was a time when large numbers of young men entered aviation training, and the impetus for these studies came from an interest in the way they would relate to one another in leadership terms, having come recently from a college environment into a quite different institutional setting. The device most readily at hand, providing a composite of leadership choice patterns over many groups, was the sociometric measure often called a "peer nomination." Of particular note is the ready way in which this instrument permits the identification and quantification of emergent leadership.

The peer-nomination technique is given special focus in Part Three. Especially important is the way in which the technique allows a tapping of certain elements of interpersonal perception

arising from interaction. The empirical work presented in the five
chapters following indicates the diversity of use to which peer-
nomination scores can be applied, from the prediction of complex
performance criteria to the assessment of morale.

Part Four represents more recent theoretical and experimental
work on emergent leadership and its relationship in particular to
conformity and competence. Here a fuller development of the
idiosyncrasy credit model is afforded along with several experiments
bearing upon hypotheses derived from it. Thus a broadening of
interest to influence process more generally as well as a narrowing
to find the mechanisms which underlie status emergence especially
is provided. As an example, Chapter Seventeen reports one experiment in task-oriented groups in which it was found that the
time of the nonconformity by a member was a significant determinant of his ability to influence the group. His past conformity to
agreed-upon procedures was associated in general with higher influence. Conversely, early nonconformity, holding the high level of
competence constant, diminished considerably the ability to influence the group to accept what were in fact good solutions. Most
significantly, nonconformity *after* a period of initial conformity
yielded the highest level of acceptance of influence. Another example is provided in Chapter Eighteen by an experiment using a
simple "trait description" technique to simulate interaction. De-
scribing a person as more or less competent in the group's task, and
new or not new to the group, yielded systematic and significant
differences concerning the extent to which respondents would
accord a position of authority to the stimulus person. This was
found subsequently to bear a direct relationship to the degree to
which innovative behavior—as one instance, "suggests changes
from group plans"—would be disapproved if manifested by that
person. Thus, higher status yielded less disapproval of innovation
and revealed consistent response tendencies regarding sources and
effects of status even where there is no literal interaction.

This work has gained from my association with many people,
teachers, students, and colleagues. Among the latter, I especially

wish to record my debt to John T. Bair, Richard deCharms, Alvin
Gouldner, Raymond G. Hunt, Luigi Petrullo, Wilse W. Webb,
and Richard H. Willis. From our recent work together, exemplified
by the experiment reported in Chapter Nineteen, Richard H.
Willis has provided a source of stimulation for several ideas represented in the concluding chapter. Though I accept full responsibility for their formulation here, I am pleased to acknowledge
his part. I am also grateful to him and to John T. Bair and Wilse
B. Webb for allowing permission to reprint here some of our joint
efforts. To James W. Julian and Irwin Silverman I extend my
gratitude for their helpful comments on various portions of the
manuscript.

Over the period of many years, I have benefited considerably
from the sustained support of the Office of Naval Research, particularly the Group Psychology Branch of the Psychological Sciences Division. The opportunity afforded to pursue much of the
work presented here is in no small way a direct outgrowth of this
support. Among others with whom I have had past or present as-
sociations at ONR, I should like to give due recognition to Joan
Criswell, Abraham S. Levine, Howard E. Page, Luigi Petrullo,
Denzel D. Smith, and Richard Trumbull for their assistance and
good fellowship.

I wish to thank the following publishers for their co-operation in
permitting republication of a number of my papers here: the American Psychological Association; Holt, Rinehart & Winston, Inc.;
Personnel Psychology; Psychological Reports; Sociological Review;
and the Springer Publishing Company.

Not least, I am delighted to express my gratitude to Mrs.
Leonore Ganschow for her unsparing aid in the preparation of the
manuscript, and to my wife for her great helpfulness at many points
along the way.

Buffalo   E. P. H.
April 1964

Contents

IV   Leadership Emergence, Status, and Conformity, 149

I

Leadership, innovation, and influence in varying settings

The theme of this book is that leadership is a relationship between a person exerting influence and those who are influenced, and that it is best seen within the framework of group process. In this section we encounter the main guidelines which sustain this view through the balance of the chapters.

Chapter One is a broad coverage of where we stand in defining and approaching leadership events. The attempt here is to bring into focus the key ideas which shape the field, without in any sense seeking to be encyclopedic in coverage. Both historical trends and contemporary movements are shown in relationship to the work being pursued under the heading of leadership today.

From this larger view we move to some particulars in Chapter Two which reveal the special importance of emergent leadership. Relevant here is the treatment of leadership and followership phenomena in terms of interaction process rather than static qualities.

Taking account of the reality of organizational demands for leaders, Chapter Three offers some of the major ideas in thinking and research on the functioning of the imposed leader in his relationship to the work group. In that context, matters of participation, recognition, and the underlying needs for both security and independence are considered.

1

1

Leadership, innovation, and influence:
An overview

Leadership is a phenomenon of classic concern. It compels attention from many vantage points and for several strategic considerations. As a matter involving the dynamics of group behavior, it has clear antecedents in the earlier formulations of "the crowd" and "mob behavior" which enliven the work of such forebears of modern social science as Tarde, LeBon, Ross, MacDougall, and Simmel, among others. It reflects, moreover, one emphasis within the duality of social process, that is, the individual's effect on others, as a counterpart to group effects on the individual.

As a current focal point for studying influence effects from social interaction, leadership has ramifications to many other concerns relevant to group process, including conformity, morale, and social change. The study of leadership must accordingly contribute to knowledge about the dynamics of influence processes because, in a strict sense, leadership is neither a unique personal attribute, nor is it separable from social influence more generally. Speaking to this point, Thibaut and Kelley have said, "In virtually all cases, leadership seems to be analyzable in terms of other, simpler concepts ... [every] member of the group can be considered as exhibiting leadership insofar as he exercises power effectively, promotes

3

organization along functional lines, or has symbolic value" (1959, p. 289). Regarding power as such, more will be said later.

The trait approach to leadership

In the most traditional study of leadership, unique characteristics of "leaders" were sought. As is pointed out in Chapter 2, the emphasis was placed upon what "made" a leader. But this obscured some important distinctions including the source of authority and the nature of the function to be fulfilled in diverse situations. Leadership had been interwoven for so long with notions of the "man on horseback" and associated images that the more common and pedestrian, work-a-day exercise of leadership was left aside as a process unworthy of attention under the same heading.

Why an emphasis on traits should have prevailed is easy to understand. The literary, prescientific conception of the leader as a special person, a "great man," called attention to inherent qualities that one either possesses or does not, in short, "leadership traits" in the traditional usage. Illustrations of this viewpoint abound, especially in popular literature. Emerson has said, "He is great who is what he is from Nature. . . ." And Thomas Heggen, in introducing the hero of his novel about naval leadership, *Mister Roberts*, says of him: "He was a born leader; there is no other kind."

In psychology, furthermore, the trait approach found a congenial reception because of the psychologist's essential interest in individual characteristics. To measure and assess the personality of "leaders" seemed eminently appropriate to the psychologically-oriented investigator. What was overlooked, however, in the view that leaders are uniquely endowed, was the actual fact of daily life, that is, that persons function as leaders in a particular time and place, and that these are both varying and delimiting conditions; that there are several pathways to leadership, sometimes from higher authority, other times from group consent, and at times from both; and that a good many leadership events transpire routinely between individuals in reciprocal relationships, as illustrated by husband and wife, work partners, and playmates. To speak therefore of "the leader" or of leadership as if those terms conveyed an immutable "state of being" from genetics or social tradition, was to leave out a great deal of real-life social process. Indeed, if any point stands forth in the modern day view of leadership it is that leaders are made by circumstance even though some come to those circumstances better equipped than others. It is this line of development which led ultimately to the so-called "situational approach" to the study of leadership considered further in Chapter 2.

The situational approach to leadership

The distinctive asset in the situational view lies in the way it frames leadership events in the life context in which they occur. If a leader—let us take the fictional Mr. Roberts, for example—is effective, this is a relevant datum only insofar as it speaks of his setting, a ship's crew, and its associated conditions, as a time-space-person complex. His responsiveness to those men, in their circumstances, at that time, is what helps us to know and understand his effectiveness; and characteristics which make him effective there in securing a willing, responsive group support might not carry through to other situations with different demands.

It is in the nature of situational requirements that they call forth certain expectations for leadership, and these may be fulfilled by various individuals in the situation. Cartwright and Zander (1960) have put it this way: "... while certain minimal abilities are required of all leaders, these are widely distributed among nonleaders as well. Furthermore, the traits of the leader which are necessary and effective in one group or situation may be quite different from those of another leader in a different setting" (p. 492). Thus, the situational approach conceives of leadership in terms of function performed, rather than in terms of persisting traits of the leader. Closely related to this is the importance attached to the source of authority as a leader, a matter which is often discussed in terms of so-called "emergent" as contrasted with "imposed" leadership.

Emergent and imposed leadership

The distinction made in contemporary social psychology between emergent and imposed leadership has a broad significance for the nature of groups and their internal dynamics. The acceptance of influence, which is conditional upon the consent of followers, produces "emergent" leadership. "Imposed" leadership tends to be determined by superior authority; it is also possible to have an interlocking state of affairs where these reside in the same person, as in many institutions whose imposed leaders have characteristics which would make them acceptable as emergent leaders as well. In addition, much that has been learned about emergent leaders has applicability to the maintenance of status by those who are imposed leaders.

"INFORMAL" AND "FORMAL" LEADERSHIP

Another way this emergent-imposed differentiation is made is in terms of "informal" as against "formal" leadership. The former suggests emergence and the latter imposition; but using them as if they sharply defined different functions is unrealistic in light of what Homans (1961) calls "elementary social behavior," which he considers to have rules of social interaction applicable all the time. However, the terms formal and informal do have utility *not* with reference to definable modes of interaction as much as to the source of the "structure" which determines the pattern of authority of influence persons. These terms represent, in brief, situational forces rather than categories of mutually exclusive behavior.

WHAT FUNCTIONS ARE TO BE FULFILLED?

Clearly much leadership in the world is of an institutional or "imposed" variety such that task requirements are frequently set by an organization and the structure which it establishes. This means that "leaders" may be people who have highly confined, programmed functions, e.g. decision-making, within the determination of organizational constraints and expectations. This carries operational implications quite different from the usual conception of those interpersonal qualities we think of in the leader-follower relation involving freer personal interaction and "social exchange." This kind of imposed leader makes choices within tightly-limited organizational guidelines, entirely apart from being the traditional "supervisor" discussed in Chapter 3. On this point Alex Bavelas says that the *function* of the organizational leader may be definably different from his personal characteristics (1960). He suggests that in the aggregate such "leaders" are those who perform certain categories of task rather than share characteristic attributes of personality. The question in organizational leadership, says Bavelas, is not "Who is the leader?" but "What functions are to be fulfilled?" This viewpoint of common functional requirements in institutional situations reveals the expectation of an interchangeability of managerial personnel.

Interactive characteristics of leadership

Granting the demands of the situation, the question nonetheless persists whether there are characteristics of leadership which *do* cut across and pervade many situations in our society. And there appear to be some, as we suggest in Chapter 20, although they must be understood in finer detail. Gibb (1954), for example, has said that where situations are limited in certain ways leaders do exhibit various "outstanding qualifications." What these may be, and whether they refer to the task or interpersonal demands, is another matter. In either event, if these existed, that would not in and of itself contradict the potency of situational factors since their content may in fact be determined by those features of the social context which have high priority or thrust. As a case in point, competence in providing for some group function is one kind of requirement for group acceptance; but *what* that competence should be is necessarily linked to the social forces at work in that time and place. Because many groups operate in terms of verbal communication, it is hardly surprising that many studies should point up verbal effectiveness as an attribute of those who are leaders. Consequently, strangers brought together in a common plight may be expected to coalesce about the one among them who speaks out suggesting a course of action; on that same probability basis he also has a high likelihood of becoming influential in the sense of taking on a leadership role (cf. Riecken, 1958).

A further point to consider is that leaders must be aware of the circumstances which prevail in order to affect group activity. Where the leader is out of touch with the group's situation and its inclinations about it, he is ill-equipped to meet the expectations for action. Clearly then leaders must be attuned to what is expected of them, recognizing that they can and do initiate changes, including those in the social expectations themselves. It follows therefore that social perceptiveness is a feature that is demanded of leaders in many circumstances, but this need not be a "trait" since it has been found to be moderated by other elements. The leader's motivation and the nature of the group are among them. Also, where a person is *more* motivated to be aware of the happenings in a social context, he is more likely to perceive what is occurring. This holds true whenever persons have a desire to be accepted in a group, to use it as a model for action, or to identify with it even at a distance, as with some "reference groups." Therefore, if leaders are said to be more socially perceptive, this should be understood to involve not just a capacity for perceptiveness alone but quite likely some impelling motivation as well.

Status emergence and status maintenance

The relationships producing leadership can be further distinguished by studying the interrelated processes of status emergence, concerning factors at work in the *achievement* of influence, and status maintenance, covering those which allow the *retention* of influence. A failure to make this distinction has led to findings which appear contradictory on the face of it. These processes not only differ from one another but they also differ from the informal-formal distinction. Imposing authority and forcing compliance by followers to the formal structure does not eliminate the need for influence to be retained. Even with a mandate from above, as in most organizations, imposed leadership must also rest on the responsiveness of followers, and their willingness to comply. This is a lesson that organizationally imposed leaders learn at times with regret. The retention of leadership depends in some wise upon others' perceptions of competence and effectiveness.

STRUCTURE AND FUNCTION: PROCESS AND EFFECT

Since the idea of "structure" is central to what has been said and what follows, it is useful here to place it in the broader picture of the dynamics of groups. Toward that end, two pairs of distinctions are required: 1) *structure* and *function*; and 2) *process* and *effect*. While these terms are often used arbitrarily, more usually a group's "structure" refers to its organization including distribution of labor, status differentiation, patterns of communication, and such normative expectations as procedures, roles, and the like. On the other hand, a group's "function" refers to the activities or behaviors carried on mutually for the achievement of some common goal, reflecting the purpose or *raison d'être* of the group. Thus, structure by definition includes influence patterns, which optimally are supposed to be harmonious with the function to be fulfilled and, in turn, the goal to be commonly attained.

In the case of emergent leadership, the structure arises from the group's perception of its function, and if that function should change grossly then the structure must also be altered for the group to act effectively. Effective leadership therefore is a structural feature of the functional or task requirements presented to the group, as we point out in greater detail in Chapter 20. However, structures have a self-sustaining quality which, as will be noted, supports the maintenance of present leadership. This tendency is all the more marked in institutional settings where the structure is imposed from above, and where leadership is anchored in the prevailing structure. But in either case, whether structures are informal or formal, leaders are beneficiaries of the present structure, even though a change in situational conditions may instigate alterations in the structure. The basis for the leader's hold on the structure lies significantly in his role in molding it to his design, or to his exemplification of its associated function by his competence in a focal group task.

In the other distinction noted, group "process" may be thought of as the ongoing nature of intra-group activities, including for example goal-seeking behavior and related patterns of interaction. In an important sense, process encompasses the inter-relationship over time between function and structure. Group "effects" refer to the *products* of process, including member attitudes seen in such things as cohesiveness, or shifts in leadership expectations, or in broad social change.

INITIATING STRUCTURE

Structure is vital in, for example, Hemphill's (1958, 1961) view that leadership involves the "initiation of structure" in the group. He sees leadership not simply as a part of structure, but rather as an instrumental agent determining the shape it should take. In his terms, *attempted* leadership is based on such initiations of new structure; however, the leadership act is incomplete unless that initiation is *accepted*. A completed sequence in Hemphill's phrase is "successful leadership"; and "effective leadership" occurs when a contribution is made to the solution of the group's mutual problem. Hemphill and his co-workers, Pepinsky and Shevitz (1958), have reported at least one study where the degree of initiation of structure by a subject is significantly raised or lowered by the acceptance that person is led to believe he has, through a form of social reinforcement. This serves as a demonstration of the situational constraints or enhancements which shape leadership acts.

And most importantly, it speaks to processes which determine an individual's *attempts* at influence assertion.

On the other side of this process there is the broader issue of conditions which determine the *acceptance* of influence. Several kinds of approaches may be fruitful in highlighting one or more variables which have potency in this respect. High in contemporary interest are the interaction characteristics of leader-follower relationships. Here the focus rests upon what conditions permit acceptable assertions of influence. Several clusters of elements are bound up in this interest. One of these is the nature of the group context, suggesting variables in the group's function and structure, its cohesiveness, communication, and the like.

PERCEPTION OF THE LEADER

Also of key importance is the perception "relevant others" hold of the potential leader, the influence-person, in that setting. Considering leadership as an interpersonal encounter necessarily involving person perception, three categories of qualities appear to be in the nature of distinctions made. Though variously labeled, these are: 1) the perceived competence of the individual, broadly conceived in terms of the specific task of the group at the time; 2) the adherence of the individual to agreed upon procedures, that is, what he does to demonstrate his identification with the group; and 3) those of his personal characteristics or attributes perceived as valued for their own sake, though they may contribute less specifically to the function of the group. The first two factors appear to have prime significance in the attainment of a position of influence where emergence is possible. This suggests that the individual must be in a group sufficiently long to develop in others a degree of trust or esteem for him, and for them to note his part in helping to fulfill group goals.

While this process of status attainment goes on, the group's prevailing social forms must be adhered to, unless the potential influence person is extremely competent, or is in the category of an expert, which presents special circumstances. Generally speaking, it is unlikely that just any member of a group could achieve leadership by a suggestion for innovation very early in his exposure to a group. The context is simply not yet favorable. And this is the common observation made in connection with the newcomer to a group: he is considerably more restricted in behavior than the person who has established himself there over a longer time and has gained "idiosyncrasy credit" by proving himself.

Once attained, the maintenance of leadership requires innovation and change as acceptable, indeed often expected, functions on the part of the leader. Having accorded high acceptance to this individual, the group may receive his suggested innovations more favorably. This is related to a number of formulations, including Homans's (1961) concept of "status congruence," that is, the appropriateness of behaviors and functions in relation to hierarchical status.

Power and influence

A frequently made assumption is that influence necessarily involves the exercise of power. This would suggest that any act of influence would represent power over the person actually influenced; however, in this sense, the terms influence and power are not synonymous. Another questionable assumption is that imposed leadership, with authority vested from above, must operate in terms of the assertion of power.

There are several factors which should be borne in mind to qualify these beliefs. In the first place, power may be both influence potential as well as resistance potential as Cartwright (1949) has pointed out. Second, the absence of influence acceptance in the face of an assertion of influence does not necessarily mean that the influence agent is powerless but could mean that he does not fully assert the influence potential at his command. This matter of restraint in the use of power available in imposed organizational structures is a necessarily vital condition for smooth relationships. Where the person in authority consistently uses the full power of his position this undercuts his long-term effectiveness because of the resistance built up over time, as well as other disadvantages. Unfettered use of power obviously does occur, but a greater likelihood exists that bargaining relationships of a jointly rewarding nature will develop to offset resistance, as Thibaut and Kelley (1959) have contended in their model of social exchange.

Another consideration then is that power may be employed by degrees. It is not an all-or-nothing matter. Even in the most authoritatively oriented structures, it is not identical to exercising "effective leadership," as we note in Chapter 20. Indeed, imposed leaders must reckon with the structure of the emergent group which serves as a base of security for the individual and provides power in the form of a mutual resistance potential to the dictatorial use of power. This is by way of saying that power to avoid untrammeled exploitation rests with the work group and that this must be recognized as a counterforce by the supervisor, an essential point elaborated in Chapter 3. Even in extreme conditions, where power is founded on physical force which overdetermines the outcome, power is *not* an instrument of successful leadership in its own right.

The key consideration to be emphasized is that the influence assertions of the imposed leader are evaluated by the group in the context of the perceived motivation involved and the consequences for some common good represented in a group goal. It is in this sense that the maintenance of leadership, even by an imposed leader, requires a regard for the working relationships which are affected by assertions of power.

Social change

An expansion of these points leads to the consequential issue of social change. All societies, and the groups comprising them, must continually undergo some change as an elemental fact of nature. There are, however, forces resisting change, whatever the desirability of the new course offered. Very often these arise because of the essential security provided by the familiar. Accordingly, a central question in considering social change is how groups come to recognize that some well-entrenched social form ought to be altered. It is especially useful to employ terms associated with status emergence in pursuing this further.

For social change to be instigated there must be a comparison between things as they are and things as they might be. This suggests a flow of information through some channel of communication, and calls attention to the work on diffusion and innovation by Katz and Lazarsfeld (1955) and Menzel and Katz (1955) in which the leader is found to be a person who provides an interpretation of the world outside the immediate group. It is he who conveys a structure in terms of "social reality," and the acceptance of innovation. Partly because of this, social change no longer can be cast in the tidy terms of the venerable historical controversy of "the man *or* the times." More accurately, in contemporary social psychology, this problem seems a matter of studying the combined impact of the leader and the social context upon the view that followers will hold of their world. This is significant to their associated willingness to undertake change. In short, neither man nor the situation exists independently of the other since, in the *emergence* aspect of leadership, group members operate from the base of a situation and the particular demands it makes for "task requirements."

In a related vein, it is also true that suggestions offered are variously reacted to depending upon the status of the person from whom they come, a point already noted here and discussed further in Chapter 20. This offers a tie with balance or congruity theories of attitude change which suggest the cognitive aptness of similarly "signed" terms, i.e. leader positively signed, his recommended course of action positively signed, then "balanced." The work of Osgood and Tannenbaum (1955) and of Heider (1958), among others, is suggestive of this line of analysis. If we take the relatively simple case of the leader as a positively signed term, his neutral idea or negatively signed idea may carry the day: it is cognitively consistent for him to be identified with positive things, and so balancing occurs. Still, equally possible, a negatively signed person, or a neutral person, may gain status by espousing a potent "positive" idea with which he becomes associated and from which he then draws residual benefits.

An expansion of these considerations would lead to a somewhat richer, more nuance-laden conception of social influence involving the leader as the emitter of complex multi-signed stimuli which become relevant to the follower, as recipient, in terms of the motivational and reference group contexts of which he partakes at a given time.

The leader's emergence or waning of status is thus inextricably linked to the prevailing situation, both as group members understand it from the information at hand and as they hold attachments to persons or orientations, present but also past. A change of the influence structure must necessarily overcome the resistance which these factors erect and encourage. It is not so much, then, the "man or the times" as it appears to be the perception of the man and what he represents himself to be and to stand for in the context of the already enveloping situation. Yet, once having achieved status of high influence, what he does may not and indeed need not fit past expectations for, in the maintenance of his position, he is obliged to fulfill new expectations which arise as the situation inevitably is altered.

2

Emergent leadership and social influence

The term *leader* is used so broadly that it is best to define our use of it at the outset. In general, leader denotes an individual with a status that permits him to exercise influence over certain other individuals. Specifically, our concern is directed toward leaders deriving status from followers who may accord or withdraw it, in an essentially free interchange within a group context. Group consent is therefore a central feature in the leader-follower relationships touched on here, although this limitation does not mean that we will totally neglect the possible implications for all kinds of groups, from the simple dyad to the institutionally based formal group or society.

Primarily, our intention is to offer some observations and empirical findings which strike at the persisting notion of a dichotomy between leadership and followership. We first present some results of sociometric research, followed by a theoretical model that treats the emergence of status and assertion of influence as outputs from interaction centered in interpersonal perception. Finally, we introduce some findings from a laboratory experiment with groups to

Adapted from Chapter 3 in L. Petrullo and B. M. Bass (Eds.), *Leadership and Interpersonal Behavior,* New York, Holt, Rinehart & Winston, Inc., copyright © 1961. Reprinted with permission of the publisher.

underscore particularly conceptions from this model which concern the different effects of perceived competence and conformity on the emergence of status and the assertion of influence.

Status in general

There are different bases for status and different expectations regarding its operational features. These defy ready cataloguing, but in our usage here, status refers to the placement of an individual along a dimension, or in a hierarchy, by virtue of some criterion of value. To say that an individual has "status" does not describe an intrinsic attribute or a stable pattern of his behavior; rather it describes the relationship of that individual to certain others and their attendant behavior toward him. Interpersonal perception is a necessary part of this process.

Who perceives what about whom is of central importance not just in terms of the literal case, but also in terms of expectancies. The behavior of the object person is not seen just by itself; it is also effectively *matched* against a standard of expectation held by the perceiver. Before a status distinction can arise, therefore, two things must hold: an arousal of a socially conditioned expectancy, and a flow of information regarding the object person. The perceiver will have had some exposure to the perceived through direct experience or through secondary sources; this leads to a perceptual differentiation which underlies a shift in "behavior toward."

Granting, as an example, that a millionaire possesses a fairly uniform degree of higher status in our society, he operates without it if unshaven, unkempt, and unknown, he moves about among strangers. Even though an economic criterion and an expectancy already exist for a status distinction, the relevant information is absent. In this instance, the emergence of status is linked to one kind of standard, though a wide variety of others could apply (Hyman, 1942). What the relative impact of these will be resides in complex issues of value. In any case, status is not a sole and stable function of some given feature of social interaction between

two particular individuals. Cross-pressures of time and place affect
the balance.

If leaders occupy a given status relative to followers, this is one
function of the way the former are at some moment perceived and
reacted to by the latter. Gibb (1954, p. 915) has made the point
this way: "Followers subordinate themselves, not to an individual
whom they perceive as utterly different, but to a member of their
group who has superiority at this time and whom they perceive
to be fundamentally the same as they are, and who may, at other
times, be prepared to follow." Being a follower is not inconsistent
with being a leader, in time. This begs the question of the persisting dichotomy, so some history may be useful here.

The changing approach to leadership

The tradition of concern and controversy about leadership extends
far back into the history of social philosophy. This was to stamp
related empirical work with a decided bent toward enumerating
qualities of the leader. While recent research has seen the leader
displaced from this traditional position at center-stage, not very
long ago it was typical to indulge in a quest for broad traits of
leadership.

Though essentially a matter of emphasis, as in the work of Cowley (1931), traits were selected without regard for situational variants. Gradually a useful distinction between appointed leaders and
those who emerged through the willing response of followers was
recognized. This was partly a reaction to the burgeoning interest
in informal groups with their self-generating status hierarchies, and
partly a result of the accessibility of sociometric devices which provided means for studying the consensual choice patterns of various
groups.

During this phase, popularity as a feature of group-emergent
leadership was given disproportionate importance. Much of the
earlier sociometric work equated choice as a roommate or study
companion with choice as a leader, and several well-known and

substantial studies gave credence to this presumed parity, though only within a limited context (for example, Jennings, 1943).

Eventually, both the trait and popularity emphases were subordinated to an approach which focused on the varying demands for leadership imposed by an immediate situation (Hemphill, 1949; Carter, Haythorn, Shriver, and Lanzetta, 1951). The literature survey by Stogdill (1948) on personal factors associated with leadership was quite decisive in pointing up the disordered state of the earlier viewpoint, which disregarded situations. It was not as though the situational view prevailed entirely, however; influential as it was, the literature reflected some dissent (Gibb, 1950; Bell and French, 1950). We have this appropriate comment by Gouldner (1950, p. 13): "The group contexts of leadership must be specified if a formalism sterile of action utility is to be avoided. Leadership must be examined in specific kinds of situations, facing distinctive problems. The opposite shortcoming must also be detoured; in other words, the similarities among *some* leadership situations or problems must be emphasized. Failure to do so would enmesh our investigation in an infinite analysis of unique situations as devoid of practical potentiality as the formalist approach."

Still another refinement within the situational framework was an awareness that followers define a situation in responding to leadership; they are not passive creatures of a frozen social matrix. Of his research on the follower as an alert participant, F. H. Sanford (1950, p. 4) has said: "There is some justification for regarding the follower as the most crucial factor in any leadership event and for arguing that research directed at the follower will eventually yield a handsome payoff. Not only is it the follower who accepts or rejects leadership, but it is the follower who *perceives* both the leader and the situation and who reacts in terms of what he perceives. And what he perceives may be, to an important degree, a function of his own motivations, frames of reference, and 'readinesses.'"

Thus it is seen, several viewpoints have been held concerning leadership and followership: first, a search for characteristics of the leader on the supposition that there is some universality among these; second, a concern with group-emergent leadership where popularity among followers may be of significance; third, a focus upon situational factors that determine, or program, the demands made upon leadership and for leadership; and finally, an interest in the more subtle interplay of motives and perceptions between followers and their leaders.

If any current leaning is discernible, it seems to be toward a focus upon the interaction between individuals and its relation to influence assertion and acceptance. In this way, we are becoming more acute in noting how interpersonal perception affects and is affected by status differentiation, as shown, for example, in the work of Jones and deCharms (1957), Dittes and Kelley (1957), and the research reported here in Chapter 18.

While it is true that two individuals may bear a stable relationship to one another in a given situation, the demands made upon them in a changing situation could reasonably alter their interpersonal behavior, assuming the necessary volitional conditions; being a leader or follower through the course of time or within a given group setting is not then a fixed state. The context for study consequently becomes more than the immediate situation in which interactions occur, since it includes the past interactions of the parties involved and their impressions of each other as well. The development of newer sociometric approaches has abetted this focus.

Sociometric techniques in the study of leadership

Leadership and interpersonal attraction have been studied more by sociometric techniques than in any other way. It is useful, therefore, to note in perspective the changing complexion of the service these techniques have provided. In early work with the sociogram the essential thing was the interpersonal choice pattern, especially in indicating group members to be isolates or stars. In time, scores were generated through the adaptation of peer nomination as one kind of peer-rating procedure for evaluation (cf. Hollander, 1954;

and 1954b). This approach, which makes it possible to derive useful indexes of a person's qualities as seen by his fellow group members, is discussed more fully in Chapter 8 here.

A significant parallel development centers about the attempt to determine the basis for group members' perceptions of one another. This extension answers questions regarding the locus of evaluation—whether in the perceiver, the perceived, the situation in which they are immersed, or various possible combinations and weightings of these. Use of sociometric techniques in this more analytic fashion exposes bases for interpersonal attraction and reciprocal choice (Tagiuri, 1952). For the simple case of two persons interacting, attraction is often attributed to a similarity of perception (cf. Homans, 1950; Newcomb, 1956 and 1961). The literature on complementary roles bears out the contention that a common frame of reference, some commerce of understanding, disposes toward interpersonal attraction (Mead, 1934). Thus, in the simplest case of friendship formation, mutually reinforcing patterns of behavior derive from a shared perception or attitude.

For several reasons, though, it is mistaken to take this as a direct paradigm of leadership choice. Jennings (1947) has made a useful distinction in this vein, that between "psyche-tele" attraction directed by personal feelings, and "socio-tele" attraction governed at least in part by a group standard. The chooser is of course the interpreter of this standard. Nevertheless, a greater degree of restraint is introduced into the process of choice by imposing this group set. The situational demands of the group or encompassing institution have a discernible impact on the chooser, as is evident from sociometric analysis. Thus, depending upon the context, members of a group do indeed distinguish between those they like as friends and those they would wish to have as a leader, and this has been amply demonstrated in a number of studies. In one such study, reported in Chapter 12, the friendship choices of officer candidates at the Newport OCS were found to be related variously to choices for other positively loaded continua, that is "leadership qualities," "probability of success in OCS," and "interest in and enthusiasm for training." Simply liking an individual did not mean a positive evaluation of him so far as these other characteristics were concerned. A counterpart of this finding occurs in the laboratory work of Bales and Slater (1955), among others.

The traditions of sociometry set limits, however, on our understanding of leadership and followership. We continue to find, for instance, the supposition of an identity between leadership and such criteria as "want to study with" or "want to play with." Their utility for pinpointing leadership in the influence sense is questionable. In this regard, Criswell (1949) has noted that these "sets" involve choice in the face of some expectation of reciprocation, thus making mutuality important; leadership choice makes it less important. Generally speaking, whether the leader chooses those who choose him is quite irrelevant to the more central consideration of the *frequency* with which he is chosen by others.

A collateral issue has to do with the criteria set for leadership and the extent to which these are rigorously specified within an operational setting. If we conceive of the leader's influence in terms of a continuum of power, then we may have a *low* power loading, as in the case of "lead this group in a discussion," or a *high* power loading, as in "command this squad in combat." Though an obvious distinction, it has too often been plainly absent from research; one suspects that a push is made for "some measure of leadership" or a "sociometric," and anything at hand or easily concocted gets used. No wonder then that the potential follower, asked to make an evaluation, seeks in vain for a meaningful frame of reference, and then either haphazardly makes a choice or bases his decision on some abstract orientation toward the class called "leaders."

These particulars are directed only incidentally at clarifying the use of sociometric techniques, a matter taken up in greater detail in Chapter 8. More to the point here are the related and troublesome rubrics that still pervade the study of leadership. One of the more basic of these holds that some members of the group are perceived to have qualities appropriate to leadership and thus are frequent choices for that status. This may be referred to as the "pyramid model," with its peak comprised of leaders and its base of followers; it also may be reduced to a simple continuum from those of high choice, presumed to be leaders, to those of less choice, presumed to be followers. In either case, the assumption is implicit that there exists a universe of peers among which individuals, placed in the vantage point of followers, differentiate others perceived to be leaders. Followership thus becomes defined by sheer exclusion.

But supposing followership to be more active than passive, this would hardly prove an adequate basis for its appraisal. Is the follower, after all, just someone who is *not* a leader? To really pursue this one should invert the usual question of "whom to follow?" so as to render it "whom to have follow?" Group members thus placed in the position of leader would be called upon accordingly to differentiate individuals regarding characteristics appropriate to followers.

If the pyramid or continuum models are sound, one would expect that such an inversion of procedure would yield a diffusion of choice reflecting the operation of a friendship variable, or at least it should be so if followers are mainly friends. This might mean that some of the individuals otherwise selected as leaders would also be selected as followers, though on the whole one would expect that leaders should have a relatively lower standing on followership than the average standing for group members.

Research findings on the pyramid model

A study taking account of the aforementioned points was reported by the author with Webb in 1955 and is presented in Chapter 6. Prominent among the considerations prompting that research was the view that the traditional sociometric model of leadership and followership might be open to challenge. Since our procedure followed closely the approach discussed, our data serve to address the issue squarely.

Eight sections of aviation cadets (total $N = 187$) were asked to complete three peer nominations upon graduation from a sixteen-week preflight course at Pensacola. The first two of these were on leadership and followership, the third on friendship. On both the leadership and followership form each cadet was asked to assume that he was assigned to "a special military unit with an undisclosed mission." Then, for leadership, he was directed to nominate in order three cadets from his section whom he considered best qualified to lead this special unit and three cadets from his section whom he considered least qualified. A similar set was presented for followership with the instruction that the cadet assume that *he himself had been assigned to the leadership* of this special unit; from among the members of his section, he was instructed to nominate three cadets whom he would want as part of his unit and three whom he would not want.

Correlational analysis revealed leadership and followership nominations to be related to a high degree, $r = .92$. Friendship had a significantly higher relationship with followership, $r = .55$, than with leadership, $r = .47$. But apart from this, friendship nominations were not found to bear appreciably on the basic leadership-followership relationship. Of the three friendship nominees designated by each subject, an average of more than two were not mentioned at all in the leadership nominations made by these same subjects.

One further finding deserves attention in light of the previous remarks. If, as has been contended here, followership may be studied in terms of the desires of potential leaders, then a reasonable question is whether actual status on the leadership continuum renders a difference in followership choice. An analysis then correlated the followership scores derived from nominations made by individuals in the top half and by those in the bottom half of the leadership score distribution. Its value for followership scores independently summed from these two nominator segments was .82 It would seem therefore that chooser status did not make an appreciable difference in the choice of followers within these groups

On this the results were clear: the more desired followers tended to be chosen from the upper extremes of the leadership distribution; indeed, the correspondence was marked. Furthermore, the influence of friendship, so often taken for leadership under the heading of "popularity," had little effect on this relationship.

In a later study by Kubany (1957) quite comparable results were found with medical school *graduating seniors* ($N = 87$). A high correlation obtained between peer-nomination scores for choices on "family physician" and "turn over practice to" ($r = .85$). Neither of these were as highly correlated with "friend and social associate," and each was differentially correlated with peer-nomination scores for professional knowledge, skill, and favorable interpersonal behaviors, with professional knowledge and skill typifying more closely the "family physician" choice. We may consider that where one physician is prepared to give himself over to another for his own personal care and that of his family, the latter may be viewed as a leader. Though operating within a professional relationship, his influence in interpersonal relations may be quite real; therefore, choices for "family physician" betray a view of the individual more in keeping with leadership. On the other hand, when one physician sees another as someone to whom he would "turn over his practice," this signifies a disposition more in line with followership since the chooser says in effect that this is someone whom he believes would take his directions and conscientiously fulfill them as a self-surrogate (Hollander, 1958b).

These data bolster the previous findings, but mainly in highlighting competence as a valued feature in a multiplicity of joint work situations. That individuals should choose potential leaders as those whom they would also wish to have as followers is not in itself surprising. For one thing, institutional hierarchies plainly create such demands, so that responding well as a follower is apt to be demanded at all levels. Common areas of competence are to be expected, but more important is the way in which competence may contribute to the development of leadership status, particularly when combined with still other interpersonal characteristics. Beyond one's ability at the task, followership holds an incipient state of leadership. Consequently, any model of leadership is deficient if it fails to account for transitions in status, especially as these are occasioned through the time-linked features of interaction.

Some implications of emergent status

The findings amassed suggest that two things in particular are important in an individual's attainment of leadership. First, that he be seen as competent in the group's central task; and second, that broadly speaking he be perceived as a member of the group—what Brown (1936) has called "membership character."

Any group member is bound by certain expectancies—whether norms or roles—which prevail at a given time. To directly challenge these would very likely limit his upward mobility, unless a person were extremely competent and, what is more important, widely perceived as such. In most instances, adherence to the prevailing expectancies of the group is essential for the group member's acceptance. We are in effect speaking then of conformity, but not in the usual sense of fixed behavioral norms to which all group members are expected to display manifest allegiance. We conceive of conformity in terms of *group expectancies* which may be person-specific and fluid or more generally applicable and static. Thus, what may be perceived to be nonconforming behavior for one group member may not be so perceived for another. Moreover, this is a function of status accumulated from past interactions, and is taken up more fully in Chapter 15 where we present the construct *idiosyncrasy credit* to refer to status as a summative consequence of being perceived by others as contributing to the group's task and living up to expectancies applicable at any given time. These "credits" are in essence positively disposed impressions of a person held by others; operationally, they provide the basis for influence assertion and its acceptance. The apparent paradox that leaders are said to be at once innovators and also to be conformers to group norms may be seen therefore as a matter of sequence.

So long as the person does not lose credits by sharp breaks with a past record of competence and conformity to expectancies, he rises to a level of credit which permits deviation from, and even open challenge of, prevailing social patterns of the group. In attaining this level, however, the particular expectancies applicable to him will have undergone change, so that it may be less appropriate to behave in the same way.

Guided by this credit model, an experiment with problem-solving groups was conceived to test the effects upon influence acceptance produced by the nonconformity to procedural norms of a confederate of the experimenter who was very competent in the task. It is reported in Chapter 17.

The key manipulation in that experiment was nonconformity by the confederate, through various zones of five trials each, to procedures previously agreed upon by the group in a pre-trial discussion. The fifteen trials were considered as three zones—early, middle, and late—with the discussion taken to be part of the first zone. A group choice, whether by majority rule or otherwise (this determined by the group) was required for each trial, following the three minutes permitted for considering alternatives. At the conclusion of each trial, the experimenter announced the outcome, that is, a negative or positive sum of varying magnitudes representing funds won or lost.

Six treatments were used: nonconformity throughout; nonconformity for the first two zones; for just the first zone alone; for the last two zones; for just the last zone alone; and not at all, as a control condition. Each subject was heard to report his recommended choice at least once during every one of the trials. Had it been *accepted* by the group as its own, the choice recommended by the confederate would have yielded the higher payoffs on all but four trials.

In the zones calling for nonconformity, the confederate violated procedures by speaking out of prescribed turn, by questioning the utility of majority rule, and by unsupported—but not harsh—challenges to the recommendations made by others. He manifested such behaviors on an approximate frequency of at least one per trial with a mean of two per trial considered optimum. Thus, he would break in with his choice immediately after an earlier respondent had spoken and before the next in sequence could do so; when there were periods of silence during a trial, he would observe aloud that maybe majority rule didn't work so well; and he would show a lack of enthusiasm for the choice offered by various others on the matter of basis.

The findings revealed the ongoing effect of task competence in increasing influence acceptance over time, seen in the rising means across zones. While current nonconformity does not yield a significant effect, past nonconformity does. In those groups where the confederate began nonconforming after the first zone, both his suggestions and nonconformity were accepted with minimal challenge; by the third zone, his suggestion that majority rule was faulty typically netted a rubber-stamping of his choice. Again, if he had already accrued credit, the pattern of interrupting people out of turn was simply imitated by others. However, where he exhibited nonconformity from the outset, quite opposite effects were elicited from the others, notably with comments of censure.

Summary

In this chapter we have considered variables yielding emergent status in terms of potential influence. It has been shown that social interaction gives rise to a kind of interpersonal assessment, and that this is made up of task-related elements and behaviors matched by the perceiver against some social standard, referred to here as an "expectancy."

Where an individual fulfills these conditions of competence and an adherence to group expectancies over time, he is said to have accumulated "idiosyncrasy credits" and, at some threshold, these credits permit innovation in the group as one evidence of social influence. Thus the task-competent follower who conforms to the common expectancies of the group at one stage may emerge as the leader at the next stage. Correspondingly, the leader who fails to fulfill the expectancies associated with his position of influence may lose credits among his followers and be replaced by one of them. Which person achieves and retains leadership will therefore depend upon the perceptions of others from ongoing social interaction.

3

The organizational leader and the
work group

The problem of the organizational leader is that though he has power, it alone does not command responsive group support. The imposition of authority, as we noted in Chapter 1, is not sufficient to insure loyalty and ready acceptance of influence. Work groups in all kinds of organizational settings are likely to generate a structure which accords a place of some authority to emergent leaders. Though this need not be a source of conflict with imposed authority, smoothly functioning relationships require that this "structure" and its functions be understood by the organizational leader for him to be fully effective. This fact is not the same as just contending that "good human relations" are desirable, since by itself that phrase omits a great deal else of importance. What is meant is that patterns of social relationships are of justifiable interest to the organizational leader.

People at work, it is well to remember, are still fully dimensional. They bring with them more than their laboring efforts; they also bring their social selves. And they find more than an opportunity to secure financial remuneration there since the work setting represents the potential for social rewards in the intangible form of recognition and participation. These symbolic elements are quite apart from strict dollars and cents value, and they play vital roles in producing individual behaviors and dispositions.

Any organization is a small scale social system operating in terms of two patterns of relationship. First, each person has his designated place and a designated function within the organizational whole, represented by the imposed structure formally set down on an organizational chart. But there is also a highly important informal or emergent structure established within the groupings into which people are placed to carry out their function. To handle properly the day-to-day interrelationships in a work setting it is essential that the existence of both structures be recognized by the imposed leader. This is especially so since problems of morale typically are bound up with some pattern of human relationships which stem at least indirectly from the informal structure of the work group.

Effects of the work group

Morale is a complex of attitudes toward the total experience of the work setting. Positive identification with the work group and group goals is one potent factor which serves to facilitate high morale. In this respect, morale is a psychological state of the individual which reflects his dependence upon the group for certain satisfactions and security. Rensis Likert (1956) in summarizing some of the findings obtained in field studies by Michigan's Survey Research Center accords a highly significant role to the work group in producing lower absence rates, better interpersonal relationships, more favorable attitudes toward the job and company, and higher production goals.

A large scale study by Seashore (1954) demonstrates how high cohesiveness of work groups is closely bound up with high productivity and low worker anxiety. With some six thousand employees drawn from over two hundred work groups of from five to over fifty in a machinery factory, Seashore has strong evidence for the significant impact of work group association on such relevant criteria as productivity and worker anxiety.

Though more often it is the ability of work groups to restrict output which is described, the opposite end may be served as well. Kahn and Katz (1953), studying over two thousand employees in a large insurance company, report that one of the four major variables consistently related to the productivity of an organizational group and to the psychological returns secured by its members was the amount of *pride in work group.*

Research by Van Zelst (1952) illustrates how production may be increased and social relationships made smoother by permitting workers to select individuals with whom they wish to work. He made use of a sociometric technique whereby each worker chose his work partner. The subjects of this experiment were carpenters and bricklayers who had worked with each other for over five months and thus knew each other well. In addition to raising productivity, there was also an increase in ". . . the worker's sense of satisfaction and participation through an increase in his interest in liking of his job, the removal of anxiety due to friction between work partners and the creation of a friendly, cooperative atmosphere" (p. 184).

It seems clear, then, that the work group produces relationships which bear on several important outcomes relating to productivity and individual satisfactions. From this fact stems a number of challenges to the organizational supervisor, the "imposed leader," who must direct the activities of the work group.

Security and independence

Some years ago McGregor (1944) in discussing several features of industrial leadership concluded that security and independence are two basic needs which people fulfill in organizations. Security, he notes, cannot be accorded simply by making provisions for retirement, for insurance, or for guaranteed wages; it must be established by the creation of the proper atmosphere, something in the manner and attitude of superiors, a leadership climate. A significant aspect of that climate is what we have called "structure," in such particulars as these: knowing what is expected and having some awareness of how one is doing; consistent discipline in supporting the right and correcting the wrong; and foretelling changes that may affect personal welfare. Seen in this light, security thus becomes a prerequisite for independence. Once given a sense of security established in relationships to superiors, and an opportunity to share in discussing problems and actions which may affect the employee, a greater sense of independence prevails.

The view McGregor puts forth has particular implications for the style of leadership which permits participation by subordinates. A simple extrapolation would be this: given a clearly defined structure as a basic characteristic of the social climate, participation enhances the person's sense of security in that he gains some control over the social mechanisms in his environment. Furthermore, his participation within the work group increases the person's sense of recognition as an individual in his own right, thus providing also for his independence. This appears to be a "style" of supervision which maximizes utilization of the work group as an entity with its own structural properties shared by its members.

What implications does this have for supervisors? One fact of life that Likert (1961) has pointed out is that supervisors tend to practice the same pattern of supervision they experience, that it is an organizational characteristic to be, as he puts it, "employee-centered" or "job-centered" in supervision. Evidently this distinction is meaningful in terms of morale. Likert reports that high morale groups more frequently describe their supervisor's activities by indicating his interest in the well-being of the employees by such acts as recommending promotions, transfers, pay increases, and informing men of what is happening in the company, keeping them posted on how well they are doing, and paying heed to complaints and grievances. This pattern has been found to hold in a host of studies by the Survey Research Center in various work settings.

General supervision and close supervision have also been studied as another difference in style. Katz and others (1950) report from research on twenty-four section heads and 419 nonsupervisory employees in the home office of the Prudential Insurance Company that high producing sections were significantly more likely to receive general rather than close supervision from their superiors. With high producing sections, there also tended to be a higher degree of employee-orientation than production-orientation. From studying a sample of 298 workers and 72 foremen on the Chesapeake and Ohio Railroad, Katz, *et al.* (1951) report that the foremen of high productivity groups seem more secure about their standing with their own supervisors, feel less pressure, and are more satisfied with the amount of authority they have than are foremen of low productivity groups.

In their large scale study involving over 2000 employees in an insurance company, Kahn and Katz (1953) found that supervisors with the better production records devoted more time to planning work and performing special skilled tasks. Also they gave a larger proportion of their time to supervisory functions, especially to the interpersonal aspects of their jobs. Low producing supervisors checked up on their employees with far greater frequency in order to give them more detailed and more frequent instructions.

One consequence of findings such as these is to lead some to conclude mistakenly that the supervisor's function in providing a structure should be downgraded. Apart from the absolute merits or demerits of any given structure, it seems clear that a structure is necessary to the fulfillment of stable relationships and a sense of continuity and wholeness. In short, some supervision is essential to secure stability of expectation for the people in an organization. As an example of this requirement, Arensberg and McGregor (1942) found that a cause of poor morale in the engineering department of a company which had a reputation for being an engineer's paradise was inadequate structure. Each man supposedly had almost complete freedom with no supervision other than a committee which was to approve research plans and check on progress periodically. It developed, under study, that there were indeed lines of supervision but that these were not as readily apparent as more formalized lines of authority in other organizations. The net result was that instability had been set up in what should have been an ideal environment. The workers complained that the flexibility which presumably had been accorded them yielded certain informal practices which had a decidedly limiting effect on this avowed freedom. In simplest terms, the supervisory structure which actually did exist was not as readily apparent and could not be dealt with as directly as would have been the case in an organization with more obvious supervision.

It also needs to be borne in mind that the supervisor is not successful simply by showing familiarity and interest in his employees. Pelz (1952), in a study of foremen, concludes that human relations skills alone are by no means related in a one-to-one fashion with workers' satisfaction. Pelz says that quite another significant element is the matter of influence, that is, the extent to which the foreman is able to mediate upward the point of view and desires of those whom he directs. This seems especially reasonable in very large organizations where the needs of the working line may be obscured by sheer size.

Resistance to change

A basic characteristic of social structures is that they develop certain resistances to change. This implies that a direct threat is felt by workers when a necessary change is to be implemented which will affect the prevailing organizational patterns and the associated structure of the work group. Thus, supposedly clear-cut technical changes put the security of the workers in jeopardy. They may react to this threat by signs of overt aggression toward the administration, or absenteeism, or pretended submissiveness, or sloppy effort. A number of courses of action are open to mitigate this state of affairs, particularly participation. Before considering that more fully, let us look for a moment at the social side of technical change.

Paul Lawrence (1954), writing in the *Harvard Business Review*, disputes the position that people resist technical change as such. What employees actually resist is not technical change but social change, the change in human relationships that generally accompanies technical change. He points out that executives and staff experts need a real *understanding* of the specific social arrangements that will be sustained or threatened by the change or by the way in which it is introduced. This lends re-emphasis to the necessity for the supervisor to be aware of the structure and concerns represented in the work group.

One graphic illustration of this phenomenon of resistance is reported by Trist and Bamforth (1951) in connection with a shift in coal mining methods in a British mine. It had been traditional for coal to be mined by groups of two working together by loosening the coal, collecting it, and loading it on appropriate carts. For the sake of technical efficiency, a new system was introduced wherein large groups of forty or more individuals, operating in specialized shifts, separated these functions and thus brought about a higher level of specialization among the workers. Under the new system, absenteeism, lowered output, and other undesirable consequences resulted. Clearly, the social situation had changed in such a way as to deprive individuals of their place in a small group with which they had identified. When the investigators analyzed the situation with regard to the previous and new structure they recognized the necessity of enhancing the new group to cut down individual feelings of isolation in the mass, i.e. a lack of security and loss of independence. By training members in a variety of tasks to provide them with greater flexibility on the job, the worker's concept of his job status was elevated.

In one of the series of studies at the Harwood Manufacturing Company, Marrow (1957) was concerned with the problem of aggression and decreased efficiency arising from necessary transfers within the organization. The problem was attacked on the hypothesis that such transfers were viewed by employees as a sign of reduction of personal independence leading to a feeling of loss of face and failure. Four groups of operators were selected for study. Three of these groups were allowed to participate in the planning of transfers and were also told the reasons for the importance of these administrative changes. A fourth group continued to follow management's orders with little or no understanding of the reasons why. Marrow found the groups that were allowed participation reached their pre-transfer level of production the second day after the change and later even surpassed it; there were no quits or grievances. For the nonconsulted group, there were no signs of recovery of production level by the end of the experiment, and there were quits, aggression, and manifest lack of cooperation. Few studies are as pointed as this in illustrating the significance to the employee, and ultimately to the company itself, of an understanding of the reasons for a change in structure.

Walker and Marriott (1951), from a study of 976 men in two mass production factories and six metal rolling mills, report that attempts by supervisors to introduce variety in jobs by well-intentioned rotation of personnel, met with considerable reluctance from the workers. The authors suggest that the reasons for this reluctance stem from such factors as familiarity with the work itself, attachment to the work group, and, perhaps, to loss of earnings. Here, again, a deprivation of the former familiar structure is evident.

This resentment against management may have rather marked consequences as was found in a study by Coch and French (1948). They were concerned with retraining problems in the textile industry, and observed that the relearning period for operators transferred to a new method was significantly longer than the learning period for operators just hired for the same job. An investigation into the reasons for this phenomenon led to the conclusion that the workers were inhibited in relearning as a result of resentment against management for the initial transfer, resistance to the standard rate which had been established, and the presence of a highly organized set of group standards representing an informal structure.

These studies highlight the consideration that the manner in which a change is presented to people will have decisive consequences not only in attitudinal changes but also regarding effects on production and related considerations. In confronting this implicit problem, the technique of participation has been found to produce success in bringing about such changes on a sounder psychological basis.

Participation

Participation in organizational activities is one way the supervisor can affect worker security by engendering a feeling that the worker is an active member of his work group, and that his views and assistance are needed and recognized as important to organizational goals. Especially important is the sense this conveys that the worker has some mastery over his environment.

The use of the participation technique has already been noted in connection with the Harwood study mentioned above. In another study of this same organization, conducted by Marrow and French (1945), the problem concerned attitudes of supervisors themselves toward the integration and acceptance of older women workers. Though admitting that certain older workers were among their best, and recognizing the acute need for them, the supervisors had been balking at hiring older women. Meetings with the supervisors to discuss the origin of their stereotyped ideas about older women workers were arranged. In these sessions, it was possible to have supervisors give voice to the biases they held. Once exposed to view and discussion, these attitudes diminished in their potency and the women were accepted.

Jacobson (1951) conducted a research project involving workers in an automobile factory. With a sample of some 450 workers he carried on interviews to ascertain the degree to which they were allowed to take part in decision-making. He also was concerned with the degree to which they accepted management or union goals as their own. As part of this procedure appropriate foremen and stewards were also interviewed. The project revealed that where *both* the foremen and stewards were active in involving the workers in decisions, the men were more favorable in their attitudes toward management. On the other hand, where the steward was active in involving the men and the foreman did not involve them they tended to be higher in union loyalty and relatively low on allegiance to management goals. Further, it was found that about half as many foremen as stewards reported that they made an active effort to involve their men in a decision process, and this in part is attributable to the more emergent nature of selection as a shop steward. Most workers, as might be anticipated, felt that both the foreman and the steward *should* involve them in making decisions. On the whole, this study indicates that positive company attitudes are related to the opportunity afforded the worker to take part in decisions affecting him. It also points up the matter of worker loyalty as between the union on the one hand and management on the other. In this respect, Purcell (1960) in a study of 202 workers in the Swift and Company Packing House, including foremen and union leaders, found that loyalty to both company and union existed simultaneously to the extent that 73 per cent of the employees indicated positive loyalties to both institutions.

Still another point related to participation emerges from a summary presented by Schwab (1952) of the work done for the Detroit Edison Company by the Institute for Social Research. He finds that in order for participation to be effective in an organization it must be experienced at every level of that organization. It is part of the leadership climate. Where meetings were held of both supervisors and employees to consider problems of discipline, hospitalization, complaints, safety, transfer and promotion, retirement, and absence policy, workers expressed far greater willingness to accept new methods and to make these more effective. Most significantly, those participating indicated that they felt more security by the recognition they received through having a part in determining matters affecting their own jobs. In this same study it was found that effective utilization could be made of a so-called "feed-back" of attitude survey results to the members of a participating department. Both supervisors and employees themselves expressed the view that the group discussions employed had resulted in an increase in their job interest.

Similar evidence comes from a study carried on by Cantor (1951). Here groups of workers were invited to participate in discussions to air their problems and to make decisions concerning production rates. Trained group discussion leaders were utilized to create an atmosphere in which the workers felt free to express themselves, but these leaders did not themselves introduce the important or desirable solutions. From these conferences a production criterion was developed which the workers themselves felt they had created. Production thereupon increased. Cantor concludes by noting that production was a direct function of the worker's attitudes; when these attitudes were altered through the decision-making process, the increase in production was almost inevitable, because of the personal involvement of the workers.

Substantially identical results have been reported in other spheres, for example, among housewives who during World War II were being encouraged to make use of meat products normally considered undesirable. Lewin (1947) found with such groups that the participation technique yielded action, in the sense of making use of these meat products following the meetings, with a far greater frequency than was yielded by a straightforward lecture to similar groups.

The results from the participation studies have been among the most consistent in the area of the social psychology of work. French and Zander (1949) have explained the success in terms of two major factors: first, the view that people should not be treated as means but rather as ends, and that accordingly the functioning of a social institution should be judged ultimately by its service to the development of each member person; second, the practical statement that any social policy, decision, or solution to a problem is *more likely* to achieve its purpose if it represents a composite of the unique views, experiences, and needs of the person and the group concerned. As a final note, Lawrence (1954) points out that participation will never work so long as it is contrived merely as a device to get somebody else to do what you want him to do.

II

Leadership and interaction in formal structures

The preceding section has established some points of reference for studying leadership of both the emergent and imposed varieties. In this section, each of the chapters provides research bearing upon interaction or its outcomes in imposed structures.

Chapter Four reveals that personal authoritarianism is related negatively to selection as a leader by potential followers in a military setting. Even in an organizational structure providing for highly formalized relationships, attitudes of an authoritarian sort, measured by the F Scale, are less likely to make one a positive choice for leadership roles among potential followers. Some of the reasons for this have been suggested in the foregoing section and are further elaborated in that chapter.

A point growing out of this chapter leads to the study reported in Chapter Five. Here the question has regard to attitudes toward authority as determiners of motivation among naval aviation cadets in the same organizational structure. The results suggest that attitudes brought to the institution from past experience with authority do have a bearing upon relationships with influence-persons there.

Chapter Six reveals the close relationship between a positive assessment of those valued for leadership functions and those for followership functions where military cadets are given a free choice. Leadership in general is not found to correspond in a direct way with friendship ties.

In Chapter Seven the concern is with similarity of values and attraction to the group, defined in terms of trainee sections within the setting of the Newport Naval OCS. In the groups more attractive to members, a greater mutual perception of similarity to fellow group members is found. This sustains some of the considerations noted previously regarding work groups, despite the obvious fact that there are demarcations making trainee sections different from truly functional groups.

4

Authoritarianism and leadership choice in a military setting

Since the publication of *The Authoritarian Personality* (Adorno, *et al.*, 1950), a spate of studies has been reported in which scores derived from the F Scale or one of its modifications have been related to a variety of cognitive, behavioral, or social criteria (see Titus & Hollander, 1957). Paralleling this development, the influence of situational determinants of leadership has received heightened emphasis in the literature (e.g. Jenkins, 1947; Stogdill, 1948; Hemphill, 1949). A number of recent reports, in particular, have sought to bring about an articulation of these two areas by relating authoritarianism, in the sense of attitudes such as those in the F Scale, to leadership emergence and followership (Sanford, 1950; Havron, *et al.*, 1951; Christie, 1952; Bass, *et al.*, 1953).

Among other evidence contained in these reports, Sanford has provided a link between authoritarianism and orientation to leadership, and Christie has established a relationship between acceptance within military trainee groups in an army basic training unit and shifts in authoritarianism scores accompanying training. The findings of these studies suggest that an individual's choice of a leader is related to the latter's authoritarianism and that, within

Adapted from the *Journal of Abnormal and Social Psychology*, 1954, 49, 365-370, with permission of the publisher, the American Psychological Association.

a military context, individuals who show an increase in their authoritarianism scores during training tend to be more readily assimilated within the organizational structure.

Problem

Within military groups, the problem centering about authoritarianism and leadership choice by peers poses at least three fundamental questions: First, is the military leadership role perceived to be authoritarian within a given military group? If so, are the more authoritarian members of the group more likely to be chosen as "military leaders" by their potential followers? Finally, is there a definable relationship between one's own authoritarianism score and the authoritarianism score of the individual who is one's leadership choice?

An answer to the first question has been tentatively provided by an exploratory study completed earlier by the author among Naval Aviation Cadets. The hypothesis tested was that the military leadership role would be perceived by these subjects to be authoritarian, within a framework provided by the F Scale. It was found that, when the cadets were given two consecutive administrations of the F Scale, the first under a conventional set and the second with instructions to respond to the scale *as though* it were "a test of military leadership potential" on which they wished to make a "good score," a significant upward shift in F scores was obtained from the first to the second administration. The hypothesis was upheld, and it was concluded that F-Scale attitudes were likely to be ascribed to the military leadership role by the subjects utilized. The two remaining questions were then investigated by the study to be reported here. The hypotheses considered were as follows: (a) that there is a significant positive relationship between scores achieved on the F Scale and choice by one's peers for a military leadership position; and (b) that there is a significant difference, with respect to F-Scale scores, between the leadership nominees of those "high" on authoritarianism and those "low" on authoritarianism.

Method

SUBJECTS

Nine consecutively formed sections of cadets at the Naval Pre-Flight School, a total N of 268, were drawn as a sample. The age range for the group was 19 to 26; its mean age was 22.1 years, with slightly more than 80 per cent of the cases falling within a range of 21 through 24. The educational level of the subjects (Ss) ranged from high school graduates to one S with six years of college training; the mean was 2.8 years of college, with approximately 86 per cent of the group having had two or more full years of college. About half of the group had had some previous enlisted service. Geographically, the process of selection operated so as to represent the major areas of this country in the study sample.

PROCEDURE

At the end of three months of training, the Ss were asked to fill out a leadership nomination form for their section on which they indicated three cadets whom they considered to be *best* qualified for the hypothetical position of "student commander," and three whom they considered to be *least* qualified. By applying appropriate plus and minus weights of 3, 2, 1 for each nomination an individual received, a leadership score was derived. At about the same time in the test administration schedule, Ss were requested to complete the F Scale. The leadership scores and F scores were then transformed to standard scores based upon the individual section. The distribution of raw F-Scale total scores was unimodal and approximately symmetrical. The mean equalled 114.01 with an SD of 20.92. There is no reason to suppose that this sample differed significantly from the California samples on which the F Scale was normed. In each case, 30 was set as the mean and 10 as the SD.

Results

The major hypothesis was tested by two analyses. The first of these, a chi-square analysis making use of the total sample distributed into categories of "high," "medium," and "low" for the two major variables, is presented in Table 1. As will be noted, the chi square was significant beyond the .05 level, with the obtained frequencies indicating a rejection of the hypothesis. In addition to

TABLE 1

Authoritarianism scores and leadership standing by criterion groups †

Authoritarianism	Leadership *			Totals
	High	Medium	Low	
High	13 (21)**	34 (31)	27 (22)	74
Medium	30 (32)	53 (47)	31 (35)	114
Low	32 (22)	25 (34)	23 (24)	80
Totals	75	112	81	268

† *High* indicates a score of .6σ or more above the section mean; *Medium* indicates a score between .5σ above and .5σ below the section mean; *Low* indicate a score of .6σ or more below the section mean.
* Chi square = 12.77; $df = 4$; $p < .05$.
** The numbers in parentheses indicate the expected frequency for each cell

this, a correlational analysis was completed between authoritarianism and leadership scores for the total sample. The correlation of −.23 secured between these variables was significant at the .01 level. Since some degree of curvilinearity was observed in the correlation plot, an eta was computed and found to be .29. The chi square test of linearity was applied, and a value which did not support the hypothesis of nonlinearity was yielded.

In a supplementary series of analyses, it was found that scores achieved by Ss on the college-level ACE test correlated negatively with the authoritarianism scores, $r = −.21$, and positively with leadership, $r = +.30$. Accordingly, a partial r was calculated between the two major study variables with intelligence held constant; $r_{AL \cdot I}$ was found to be $-.18$, a low but still significant relationship. No other variables studied, i.e. age, educational level attained, or previous military experience, were found to be related significantly to both authoritarianism and leadership. Officer-like qualities (OLQ) scores assigned by superior officers in charge of the cadets were found, however, to be correlated with the leadership scores at a level of $+.55$. On the other hand, the authoritarianism scores correlated with OLQ at a virtually zero level, $r = -.06$. Table 2 presents a matrix of the relevant intercorrelations.

TABLE 2

Intercorrelations among authoritarianism score, ACE test score, officer-like qualities score, and leadership criterion for total study sample

$(N = 268; \sigma_r = .06)$

Variables	ACE	OLQ	L. Crit.
Authoritarianism	$-.21$ **	$-.06$	$-.23$ **
ACE		$+.17$ **	$+.30$ **
OLQ			$+.55$ **

** $p < .01$.

The second hypothesis was tested by a further analysis summarized in Table 3. Those "high" on authoritarianism were compared with those "low" on authoritarianism with regard to their respective leadership nominees' scores on the authoritarianism variable. The results revealed that the authoritarianism scores of those Ss nominated "highest" on leadership, by Ss who were respectively "high" and "low" on authoritarianism, did not significantly differ from one another; this held true for the "lowest" nominees as well. It would appear, therefore, that Ss nominated as "highest" on leadership were significantly lower on authoritarianism, irrespective of the standing on authoritarianism of those making the nominations.

TABLE 3

Mean authoritarianism scores * of cadets nominated highest or lowest on leadership by cadets who were high or low on authoritarianism

Nominators	Nominees		
	Nominated "highest" on leadership	Nominated "lowest" on leadership	
High score on authoritarianism	$\overline{X} = 25.30$ $\sigma^2 = 80.06$ $N = 74$	$\overline{X} = 33.74$ $\sigma^2 = 136.97$ $N = 72$	$CR = 4.87$ $p < .001$
Low score on authoritarianism	$\overline{X} = 27.29$ $\sigma^2 = 60.60$ $N = 80$	$\overline{X} = 33.17$ $\sigma^2 = 129.55$ $N = 78$	$CR = 3.79$ $p < .001$
	$CR = 1.38$ $p > .10$	$CR = .30$ $p > .10$	

* The scores reported are based upon a standard score distribution with a mean of 30 and an SD of 10.

Discussion

The findings obtained indicate a rejection of the two hypotheses with the resultant inference that authoritarians are less acceptable, as leaders, to their fellow cadets, than are nonauthoritarians. A fundamental paradox seems to be posed here. The military institution does present an essentially authoritarian structure after all. Moreover, it may be granted that military officer indoctrinees are exposed to an authoritarian conception of military leadership,[1] and in keeping with the evidence presented above, that this cadet population tends to ascribe authoritarian attitudes to the military leadership role. Yet, in a free choice situation such as this, where

[1] Cf. M. Brewster Smith's description of the impact of OCS in *The American Soldier* (1949, p. 389).

a military leadership role is to be filled, the more authoritarian individuals are not popular choices among the trainees.[2] Indeed, precisely the reverse trend is observed. In considering this finding, there are two assumptions involved which properly might be scrutinized: (a) that Ss would act upon the *traditional* role prescriptions which others like themselves appear to recognize as bound up with the military leadership role; (b) that the acceptance of authoritarian ideology, as embodied in the F Scale, necessarily implies the manifestation of some form of authoritarian behavior.

Taking account, first, of the discrepancy between the recognition of certain role prescriptions and the actual selections for role fulfillment, one might contend that the conception of an authoritarian military leader may be anchored in an incomplete and somewhat distorted stereotype. Operationally, this stereotype might be rejected under the impact of the intimate human interactions which serve to determine leadership choice, even within a military context. A case might readily be made in support of the further contention that the individual chosen as a leader by his peers, in a military setting where rigid lines of authority are drawn, may be one who is less authoritarian in his interactions with them. Although this would appear to run contrary to the work of Lewin and his associates (1939), where internal aggression was found to characterize groups of youngsters under authoritarian rule, there may be several obvious reasons which would serve to explain this contradiction: First, cadet groups function with a high level of goal orientation; second, numerous opportunities are afforded for the release of aggression through competition with other groups; finally, there remains an open question as to the comparability of child and adult groups. Also, this relationship might be attributable to loyalties within the peer group which resist dominance behavior of the sort of which the authoritarian is presumptively capable. Thus, the authoritarian may elicit a negative response from his

---

[2] While this finding is apparently in contradiction to Christie's (1952), it is of special interest to note that his most accepted group had initially been *below* the group mean on authoritarianism.

potential followers because of his emulation of an authoritarian conception of the military leadership role.

There yet remains a question as to the reasons for the conflict between this study and that by Carter, Haythorn, *et al.* (1951) which found that participants who secured leadership status in leaderless group discussions displayed authoritarian behavior. Notice, first, that in the latter study a behavioral criterion was applied and, second, that the investigators studied discussion groups of an unstable, temporary nature. The current study simply *infers* authoritarian behavior and, in contrast, makes use of persisting "real" groups of some months' establishment. It might also be noted that Bass, McGehee, *et al.* (1953) report a significant negative, but somewhat curvilinear, relationship between F-Scale scores and leadership status in leaderless group discussions. The discrepancy between this finding and the one reported by Carter, Haythorn, *et al.* leads appropriately to a consideration of the second assumption noted in the foregoing, that is, the correspondence between authoritarian behavior in some form and the subscription to F-Scale attitudes.

Without implying any disrespect for the monumental achievement represented by *The Authoritarian Personality*, one might wish nonetheless to further examine the F Scale and the meaning of an F-Scale score. At the outset, fairness demands that consideration be given the fact that the scale's constructors were concerned with tapping the personality syndrome which would be particularly receptive to antidemocratic ideology (Adorno, *et al.*, 1950, p. 4). In this regard, they have established that the scale is related to clinical evidence of rigidity, stereotypy of thinking, moral conservatism, and the like. Moreover, the scale has been shown to correlate respectably with scales of anti-Semitism, ethnocentrism, and political-economic conservatism. Yet, withal, there exists no body of evidence which directly indicates that an acceptance of this ideology is necessarily indicative of some qualitative behavior, i.e. a traditionally conceived "authoritarian behavior." This is not to deny that behavioral differences can be inferred (as they usually are from empirical evidence. Several notable studies, among them those by Rohde (1951), Bass, McGehee, *et al.* (1953), and Scodel and Mussen (1953), support the notion that perceptible differences do exist between the behavior of "high" and "low" scorers on the F Scale. Even where the influence of intelligence is held constant, as is the case in the current study, apparent differences in the behavior of "highs" and "lows" persist. This kind of evidence, while not conclusive, cannot be dismissed lightly. But it still gains us little in our quest for the precise behavioral qualities of the extreme groups on a continuum of F-Scale scores—which means, in effect, that we cannot necessarily impute authoritarian behavior to the person who accepts F-Scale attitudes.

What may we say, then, about the individual who scores high on the F Scale? In the first place, it is apparent that these "authoritarians" are defined as such on the basis of their having agreed with some grouping of F items. Furthermore, as they stand, these items appear to be a potpourri of discredited concepts running the gamut from hokum ("some day it will probably be shown that astrology can explain a lot of things") to sanctimonious self-indulgence ("no sane, normal, decent person could ever think of hurting a close friend or relative"). When this state of affairs is taken into account, it seems reasonable to consider that the "high" scorer on the F Scale may not be so much an authoritarian, behaviorally, as he may be an individual with probable inadequacies in the sphere of social intelligence or social perception. This conception does no great disservice to the work of the California group, and it partially explains contradictions of the sort alluded to above in connection with the study by Carter, Haythorn, *et al.* (1951) on the one hand, and Bass, McGehee, *et al.* (1953) on the other. More pointedly, too, it brings into focus a likely explanation for the findings obtained in the current study.

A variety of investigations (cf. Jenkins, 1947; Stogdill, 1948) have suggested that responsiveness to the needs of others, a social facility perhaps, may constitute a relatively stable component of leadership. Also, studies completed in military units have indicated that some factor similar to "permissiveness" plays a role in determining a leader's acceptability to his followers. In this regard, particular attention is directed to a study reported in *The American Soldier* (Stouffer, *et al.*, 1949, p. 385) and to an Air Force study carried on during World War II (Cranell & Mollenkopf, 1947, p. 34). Both the enlisted and officer combat veterans questioned in these studies indicated a conception of the military leader's role which was heavily weighted in the permissive direction. Of special note was the expression of a desire for greater responsiveness to their needs, opinions, and very beings by the men appointed over them.

If it is true that the man who subscribes to the bulk of the F-Scale items is correspondingly inadequate in his social interactions, this would imply that he is ill-equipped to accept the needs of other individuals or to deal with them in a socially effective fashion. Even within the context of an essentially authoritarian institution, therefore, the "F-Scale authoritarian" may be expected to draw only a minimal following for a position of leadership. Viewing the findings within this frame of reference probably serves best to explain the fact that whether nominators were "high" or "low" on the F Scale, they tended to favor "low" scorers as military leaders.

In conclusion, then, we have seen that acceptance of authoritarian attitudes may make an individual less desirable as a military leader from the standpoint of those who may be placed in a position of followership—in this case, officer indoctrinees. Whether such free choice of a leader renders that leader effective in institutional terms remains an open question to be studied further, although there already exists some affirmative evidence (e.g. Wherry & Fryer, 1949, p. 157; Williams & Leavitt, 1947, p. 291). In this vein, additional study appears indicated as well with respect to the relationship between the acceptance of F-Scale attitudes and the manifestation of authoritarian behavior. Clearly, we are confronted with the fact that there are a variety of meanings to the descriptive term "authoritarian," i.e. an ideology, a behavior, and an institutional form. At this juncture, the reality of the matter appears to be that these meanings cannot be interchanged without attendant confusion in our research efforts.

It should be reiterated that the relationships found in this investigation are of a relatively low magnitude and that their utility for prediction is virtually nil. On the positive side, however, there remains a residual of evidence which indicates that there are personal qualities relevant to social interaction, measurable to some extent by the F Scale, which bear upon an individual's acceptability as a military leader to potential followers.

Summary

A study was undertaken to determine the relationship between F-Scale scores and leadership status among officer indoctrinees. The major hypothesis was that there would be a significant positive relationship between scores on a measure of authoritarianism and leadership acceptance by peers in a military setting.

Nine consecutive sections of cadets at the Naval Pre-Flight School, an N of 268 cases, were utilized as Ss. At the end of the third month of training, Ss filled out a leadership nomination form for their section on which they named three cadets *best* qualified for the hypothetical position of "student commander" and three who were *least* qualified. At about the same time, cadets completed the F Scale. Leadership nomination scores and authoritarianism scores were then derived for all cadets.

Correlational and chi-square analyses tested the hypothesis and indicated a significant negative relationship between authoritarianism and leadership. The correlation of $-.23$ between these variables was significant beyond the .01 level. A supplementary series of analyses focused upon the relationship of a number of other variables to the two main study variables. Intelligence, as measured by the ACE test, was found to be related significantly to both authoritarianism, $r = -.21$, and peer nominations for leadership, $r = +.30$. The significance of the negative relationship between authoritarianism and leadership persisted, however, even when the effect of intelligence was partialed. In addition to the major finding, it was found that the leadership nominees of those cadets "high" or "low" on authoritarianism did not differ significantly with respect to their authoritarianism scores. In both cases, those nominated "highest" on leadership had a significantly lower score on authoritarianism than those nominated "lowest" on leadership.

A number of tentative suggestions was offered to explain the relationships obtained. It was concluded that a high score on the F Scale might be indicative of a lack of social intelligence or social perception. Accordingly, it was suggested that individuals who are "authoritarians" in the F-Scale sense are unable to deal effectively with the needs of others and therefore tend to be rejected as leaders by potential followers. Further study aimed at pinpointing the multiple usages of the term "authoritarian" was indicated as necessary.

5

Attitudes toward authority figures as correlates of motivation among naval aviation cadets

WITH JOHN T. BAIR

The interrelationship between attitudes and motivation has already been noted by a number of observers (Cantril, 1941; Newcomb, 1950; Sherif, 1948; Thomas, 1951). In recent years, evidence of the pertinence of the attitude construct to behavioral criteria has been demonstrated best perhaps in the two-volume series entitled *The American Soldier* (Stouffer, *et al.*, 1949). Although much of the research reported in these volumes was concerned with service-induced attitudes, large segments of the work dealt with persisting attitudes derived from the serviceman's reference groups external to the service. As a generalization, it might be said that in these studies attitudes were found to be functionally significant in determining the individual soldier's orientation to military life and, accordingly, to his motivation (pp. 122-30).

Reprinted from the *Journal of Applied Psychology*, 1954, 38, 21-25, with permission of the publisher, the American Psychological Association.

Problem

This study set forth to determine whether certain attitudes which a Naval Aviation Cadet brings with him to the training program bear a relationship to his level of motivation in training. It is apparent, of course, that attitudes may be ordered in a hierarchy relative to their significance to this particular training situation. That is to say, one would hardly consider that just any attitudes would have significant relevance to motivation in this setting; on the other hand, it is apparent that attitudes toward study or discipline or flying may be of the utmost relevance. In evaluative fashion, then, one might arrive at a grouping of attitudes which are presumed to be of significance in relationship to the motivation of cadets in training. With this in mind, it was considered that the area of interpersonal attitudes would provide a fruitful area for study. In particular, it was decided that attitudes toward authority figures, in this case officer-instructors (flight and ground school), would be an appropriate beginning. The intent of the study was to derive implications for further investigations as well as to determine possible applications to selection. The basic hypothesis asserted for test was as follows: that attitudes toward authority figures would significantly differentiate between cadets of "high" and "low" motivation.

Procedure

The measurement of attitudes, like the measurement of all psychological variables, offers challenging and oftentimes unique problems. This is especially so where the attitude under scrutiny is both structurally complex and emotionally laden, in this case attitudes toward authority figures. It soon became apparent that the traditional attitude scale was inadequate and inappropriate to the measurement of an attitude such as this. As a consequence, this technique was discarded in favor of the more flexible open-ended projective questionnaire (Saenger & Proshansky, 1950).

The usefulness of this method of attitude-elicitation rests on the fact that it presents the individual with a relatively unstructured stimulus situation in which he may, with equanimity, and without being consciously aware of the process, bring forth feelings that might normally be repressed through social pressures and other forces. Thus, by the employment of this technique, the cadet who felt resentment toward an instructor might vent his feelings without fear of retribution or guilt. The advantage of such a procedure in a military setting is obvious.

In its final form the questionnaire resembled superficially the form developed by Flanagan in his studies of "critical incidents" among Air Force personnel (1948). That this was merely a resemblance should be re-emphasized, lest an erroneous impression be conveyed. The main intent of the investigation was to procure information about instructors only insofar as this information revealed the attitudes of the cadet group under study. The format of the questionnaire was essentially simple. It was presented to the subjects under conditions of anonymity with the inference that only information was being solicited. In addition, subjects were specifically asked not to divulge the names of the individuals about whom they were to write. The cover sheet of this questionnaire contained these instructions: "On each of the following pages you will be asked to write briefly about a person you have known while in the Naval Air Training Program. The instructions indicate that you are to relate just one incident which typified the attitudes and behavior which have led you to make a positive or negative judgment about this person. The incident, however, does not have to be the only one of its kind, nor must it have been the main basis for your evaluation of this person."

On the top of page one the following further instructions were given: "Think of the *best* instructor you had during Pre-Flight or Flight Training. Give *just one* incident which typified the kind of attitudes and behavior which made you feel that he was the best. What were the specific details of his behavior in that particular situation?"

On the top of page two these instructions were given: "Now think of the *worst* instructor you had during Pre-Flight or Flight Training. Here again, give *just one* incident which typified the kind of attitudes and behavior which made you feel that he was the worst. What were the specific details of his behavior in that particular situation?"

Methodologically, two points deserve clarification: first, the "best"-"worst" dichotomy was utilized in an effort to secure a degree of polarization of response which would readily yield to differential analysis; second, the instrument was administered under rigorous conditions of anonymity so as to minimize any implied threat.

For purposes of this investigation, motivation was defined operationally. Cadets of "high" motivation were considered to be those who had successfully completed the basic flight stage of the Naval Air Training Program. The program is divided into three major phases: Pre-Flight, Basic Flight, and Advanced Flight. In virtually all cases, cadets who have completed Basic have been in training for one year or more. By this time attrition is minimal and the likelihood of success is very high. Cadets of "low" motivation were those who voluntarily withdrew from the program during this stage.

During a three months' period in the fall of 1951, the questionnaire was administered to a total sample of 137 cadets classified as follows: 72 cadets who were leaving training at their own request (the "low" motivation group) and 65 cadets who had successfully completed basic flight training (the "high" motivation group). In both instances administration of the questionnaire was part of a routine check-out procedure and was usually carried on with small groups numbering five or less.

A summary comparison of the two criterion groups will be found in Table 1. With respect to age and active duty time before entering training they were quite comparable. On the whole, however, cadets dropping at their own request tended to have a significantly greater amount of formal education prior to training. This latter finding corroborates, in part, certain of the results growing out of a previous report (Bair, 1952).

Following the administration procedures, responses to the questionnaire form were abstracted so as to yield only core phraseology relevant to the instructor's behavior and the cadet's reaction to this behavior. These abstracts were thereupon transcribed on 3 × 5 cards and assigned code numbers at random so as to eliminate insofar as was possible subjective bias in the content analysis procedure which followed. Thus, at no time during the categorization of these data did the judges know the disposition of the cadet whose response was in hand.

TABLE 1

Summary comparison of motivation criterion groups with regard to age, previous education, and previous military service

	Age (years)		Education * (college semesters)		Previous active military duty (months)	
Group	Mean	S.D.	Mean	S.D.	Mean	S.D.
High motivation (successful) N = 65	22.0	1.5	3.3	2.6	21.8	13.2
Low motivation (withdrawal) N = 72	22.2	1.4	5.5	2.5	20.6	14.0

* The t test of significance for the difference between the means for the college education variable was found to be 4.89. This is significant at the 1% level of confidence.

As a next step, all of the responses to the two instructional "sets," that is, "best" and "worst" instructor, were sifted to secure descriptive elements of behavior. From these, a number of categories of behavior were developed, which subsumed behavioral elements of similar quality and as much as possible used the language of the respondents rather than that of the investigators. In every instance, these categories were developed independently of one another in terms of an either-or criterion. That is, either the behavior was described in the response or it was not. Thus, overlap was possible and, indeed, very frequently took place—but only as a result of the respondent's having mentioned more than one major behavioral element.

As a check on reliability of judgment, three independent coders were asked to discriminate one category of behavior, for each of the two instructional sets, within the total population of responses to that set. Percentages of agreement with the principal investigators and the three independent coders were computed for the response categories selected for the reliability check. All were found to reach an acceptable level. In the two categories checked, the percentages of agreement for the response category *patience* were .96, .87, and .88 for each of the independent coders; for *verbal assault* the percentages were .95, .94, and .93, respectively.

Results

Frequency of response under each major category for the two cadet groups was subjected to a chi-square analysis. Table 2 presents the findings of this procedure comparing the major categories of "best" and "worst" instructor behavior for the successful and withdrawal cadet responses. In general, Table 2 reveals that the cadets of high motivation tend to manifest attitudes toward the interpersonal quality of instructor behavior while those of low motivation, on the other hand, tend to show attitudes directed at the instructor's success or failure in his role as a teacher. Close scrutiny of this table indicates that under the "best" instructor set, cadets of the "high" motivation group responded with significantly greater frequency within the categories of *personal interest* and *patience* than did the cadets in the "low" motivation group. On the other hand, the "low" group, under this same set, responded with significantly

TABLE 2

Chi-square analysis and significance levels between the motivation criterion groups for the major response categories

| | "Best" instructor | | | |
| | Per cent * | | | |
Response category	High group (N = 65)	Low group (N = 69)	χ^2	P
Showed personal interest	75	44	12.91	<.001
Indicated patience	43	20	8.08	<.01
Used good instructional techniques	37	63	9.65	<.01
Gave extra help	9	26	6.49	<.02

| | "Worst" instructor | | | |
| | Per cent * | | | |
Response category	High group (N = 62)	Low group (N = 70)	χ^2	P
Manifested verbal assault	61	21	21.74	<.001
Used poor instructional techniques	18	40	7.83	<.01
Indicated indifference	42	37	1.22	>.30

* The N's given here for the groups represent the actual number of people in the criterion groups who responded to the "set."

greater frequency than did the "high" group within the categories *good instructional techniques* and *extra help*. Under the "worst" instructor set, the "high" motivation group reacted with significantly greater frequency than the "low" group within the category *verbal assault* and with significantly less frequency than the "low" group within the category *poor instructional techniques*. No significant difference between the groups was found within the *indifference* category, under this set.

Discussion

The results indicate that differences of attitude toward authority figures do exist between cadets of "high" and "low" motivation. The hypothesis, therefore, was substantiated. Specifically, it would appear that there is a degree of variation in identification with instructors between cadets of the two criterion groups. Indeed, it may be that this process of identification may account for the differences obtained.

While it was initially considered that the attitudes studied here were brought by the cadets to the training program, one might properly question the actual temporal relationships involved. That is, were the attitudes toward these authority figures brought to the training situation, or were they conditioned mainly by experiences in training? Another research project (Hollander & Bair, 1952) has essentially duplicated the current investigation in order to provide an answer to this question. In this study, cadets *just entering training* were given a similar questionnaire form in which they were asked to give parallel information on previously encountered authority figures, that is, high school or college instructors. The results of this study indicate quite conclusively that attitudes of the cadets who subsequently withdrew from training were similar to those of the "low" motivation group of the present study. This group tended to describe the skill or lack of skill of their high school or college instructor in his role as a teacher at a significantly higher level than did the cadets who remained in training. Thus, it appears that attitudes toward authority figures are among the attitudes persistently held by the cadets, and are related to their level of motivation in the Naval Air Training Program. On the whole, it would seem that this attitude-elicitation technique bears further scrutiny as a possible device for the assessment of motivation in a number of settings.

Summary

This paper reports on attitudes toward authority figures which discriminated between Naval Aviation Cadets of "high" and "low" motivation. The "high" motivation group consisted of 65 cadets who had successfully completed Basic Flight Training, and the "low" group consisted of 72 cadets who were withdrawing from training voluntarily. Both groups were required to complete anonymously an open-ended questionnaire form which required them to describe a sample of behavior characteristic of their "best" and "worst" officer-instructors (ground and flight). Content analyses were undertaken and frequencies for each content category were determined for both groups. The results revealed that cadets of "high" motivation tended to manifest attitudes concerning *interpersonal relationships* with their officer-instructors while the "low" group stressed *competence of the instructor in his role as a teacher*. Interpretations were suggested with respect to cadet identification with authority figures as a motivational factor in this setting.

6

Leadership, followership, and friendship

WITH WILSE B. WEBB

In recent years, the value of sociometric techniques to problems of
applied research has become increasingly apparent. In at least one
sense, attestation to this fact is provided by the volume of investigations in applied psychology which have as their core the utilization of some form of sociometric measure. This is particularly true
of the so-called peer nomination discussed more fully in Chapter 8.

Several studies completed within military groups during the past
decades have yielded provocative findings regarding the validity of
peer nominations on leadership in predicting performance criteria
considerably divorced in time from the original point at which
nominations were gathered (Williams & Leavitt, 1947; Wherry &
Fryer, 1949; Hollander, 1954a). With a view toward qualifying as
well as quantifying the relevant variables underlying this demon-
strable validity, concern has developed regarding the precise interpretations which may be drawn from sociometric leadership data.
Two problems in particular appear to be fundamental to maximiz-
ing meaning from such data. One of these is the "followership"
issue—that is, the interpretation of leadership nomination data
concerning characteristics of followership. Perhaps the most cur-

Adapted from the *Journal of Abnormal and Social Psychology*, 1955, 50, 163-
167, with permission of the publisher, the American Psychological Association.

rent implicitly held position considers that individuals nominated "low" or disregarded on leadership nominations constitute a potential followership group. This view rests largely on the assumption that leadership and followership fall at opposite poles of a status continuum. An alternative position, however, which makes no such assumption, might hypothesize this "nonleader" group to be neither desirable as leaders *nor* desirable as followers. Thus, it is probable that within given institutional structures, leadership and followership qualities are interdependent. Then too, it is likely that such differences in interpretation of leadership-followership relations which arise may stem from the particular definition of followership which one adopts; a further explication of our own position on this point is detailed below. It should be noted here, however, that we have confined ourselves to a direct concern with the specific leadership-followership relationship as it is revealed through sociometric nomination techniques. This is done with a recognition of the existence of a still broader problem of the interdependence of various sociometric status continua. Such a broader consideration is typified by the work of Lemann and Solomon (1952).

A second issue with which we are concerned is the lingering doubt that peer nominations represent much more than a "popularity contest." Here, in effect, the critic asks the pragmatic question: Are leadership nominations so much a function of "relevant" factors as they are a consequence of sheer popularity, i.e. considerations of friendship? It is worth recalling that the question of the relationship of popularity to leadership is fundamental to much sociometric research and has been given considerable attention.

Although the literature in this area cannot be encompassed within this paper, it is well recognized that multiple contributions to this problem have resulted from the beginnings provided by Moreno (1934), and the work of Jennings (1943), Criswell (1943, 1946), Northway (1940), and Lemann and Solomon (1952), among others. Because of its unique comparability to the problem and population of this current study, a particularly pertinent reference here is the work of Wherry and Fryer (1949). Reporting on their research at the Signal Corps Officer Candidate School, they contend that peer ratings on leadership yield superior predictions of performance and hence constitute something beyond, or divorced from, popularity as such. Their case is substantiated by analyses against criteria external to the ratings, with conclusions drawn inferentially from the obtained relationships. This is sound evidence, but only in one aspect. The fact remains that the qualities of popularity or friendliness determining ratings in one area may well be the common determinant of success in later performance. Complementary data drawn from a more direct approach to this question would appear to be required.

In this approach, we shall treat these problems of followership, leadership, and friendship together for several reasons. First, there is the interest in any differential effect that friendship may play in leadership and followership choices. Second, and perhaps more critically, there is the realization that if a relationship were to be found between leadership and followership, it would be desirable to know the extent to which this was a function of common characteristics rather than merely a choice of friends for common roles. The ultimate aim is to provide a somewhat more complete view of the meaning of peer nominations.

Problem

Simply put, the purpose of the present study is to define more clearly the interrelationships among sociometrically derived measures of leadership, followership, and friendship. Two typical questions of a general nature to be studied are these:

1. In what way, and to what degree, is followership related to leadership?

2. In what way, and to what degree, is friendship related to leadership, and how does this compare with the relationship, if any, between friendship and followership?

Method

The sample consisted of 187 Naval Aviation Cadets representing eight sections graduating from a 15-week pre-flight training course at Pensacola in the fall of 1953. The characteristic "OCS-type" regimen to which the cadets are exposed tends to bring about strong in-group affiliations within the sections. By the end of the pre-flight course, it is reasonable to expect that each of the cadets has had an opportunity to observe his section mates under a variety of conditions. With regard to background, it might be noted, too, that all of the cadets had had a minimum of two years of college or its equivalent and have a mean age slightly in excess of 21.

During its last week of training, each section was asked to complete three sociometric nomination forms; the first two of these were on leadership and followership, the third on friendship. In the case of the leadership and followership forms, the cadet was instructed on the sheet to assume that he was assigned to "a special military unit with an undisclosed mission." For leadership, he was asked to nominate in order *three* cadets from his section whom he considered best qualified ("high") to lead this special unit and *three* cadets from his section whom he considered least qualified ("low"). On the followership form, a similar set was presented with the instruction that the cadet assume that he *himself* had been assigned to the leadership of this special unit; he was asked to nominate *three* cadets from among his section mates whom he would want as part of his unit and *three* whom he would not want. Both forms stressed that cadets were to be selected in terms of the abilities which the *nominator* considered to be important for these roles. The third form solicited the names of *three* cadets whom the nominator considered to be his best friends within his section.

Scores on the leadership and followership variables were derived by weighting positive nominations +3, +2, and +1, and negative nominations −1, −2, and −3. An algebraic summation of these weights was then divided by the potential number of nominators in the section for any one man $(N - 1)$, thus yielding an index of a cadet's standing from $+3$ to -3 on both the leadership and followership continua. While this technique is not totally refined in that it may obscure the group's ambivalent evaluation of a given individual, it has been found to be sensitive to the identification and ordering of the higher and lower ends of the distribution. Its reliability, moreover, is quite adequate, as will be seen below. Since it is applied here to the three variables for the derivation of scores to be intercorrelated and studied in relationship to one another, it presumably serves well the function of broadly highlighting the relative magnitudes of the r's involved. Friendship nominations were treated by a simple summation of a cadet's nominations divided by $N - 1$; in this instance no signs were involved since only positive nominations were obtained. The split-half reliabilities secured for the three scores, using odd-even nominators $(N = 104)$, were as follows: leadership, .94; followership, .91; friendship, .41. The r's reported have been corrected by the Spearman-Brown prophecy formula. Because of its idiosyncratic nature, the reliability for friendship is not surprisingly low.

Analyses and results

The findings of correlational analysis are presented in Table 1. The intercorrelations of the three sociometric variables will be seen to reach a significant confidence level, with the coefficient between

TABLE 1

Intercorrelations among leadership, followership, and friendship scores

$(N = 187)$

Correlated variables	r *	p
Leadership vs. followership	.92	<.001
Leadership vs. friendship	.47	<.001
Followership vs. friendship	.55	<.001

* A significance of difference beyond the .01 level between all combinations of these coefficients was obtained.

leadership and followership ($r = .92$) attaining the highest magnitude of the three. The correlation of .47 between leadership and friendship is in accord with relationships of a similar magnitude obtained between leadership and popularity in previous studies reviewed by Stogdill (1948, p. 59). To determine the significance of the difference between the three combinations of paired correlations, the t test was applied. Computation of the standard error of the difference was accomplished through a technique suggested by Peatman (1947, p. 420) which allows for dependent samples with one array in common. As indicated, all of these differences are significant beyond the .01 level, with the obtained magnitudes indicating that friendship contributes relatively less weight to leadership than it does to followership. A partial r calculated between leadership and followership, with friendship held constant, yields a coefficient of .90. Therefore, the effect of friendship on the basic leadership-followership relationship appears to be negligible.

Since the nomination scores were group-derived, with weightings introduced which might serve to obscure personal interactions, two additional analyses were completed with direct utilization of individual choice-response patterns. These are summarized simply in Tables 2 and 3. Both of these tables represent the ultimate distillation of full-scale interaction matrices. In Table 2 consideration is

TABLE 2

Mean frequency of distribution of high and low leadership nominations on followership

($N = 187$)

Leadership	Followership			Sum of means
	High	Not mentioned	Low	
Nominated high	$M = 1.67$	$M = 1.31$	$M = .02$	3.00
	$\sigma = .75$	$\sigma = .74$	$\sigma = .16$	
Nominated low	$M = 0$	$M = 1.06$	$M = 1.94$	3.00
	$\sigma = 0$	$\sigma = .79$	$\sigma = .79$	

given to the disposition of a nominator's three high and three low leadership choices, so far as his nominations for followership are concerned. The analysis questions whether a nominator tends to choose his high leadership nominees as high on followership, and whether the reverse holds true as well. Reading across the top row, the mean in each cell represents the mean number of all the nominators' three high leadership choices who were chosen high or low or not mentioned on followership. The sum of these means across will equal 3.00. Consider, as an illustration, the first cell; the mean of 1.67 indicates that this number, out of *three* high leadership nominees, were nominated—on the average—as high on followership. An alternative way of viewing these data is in percentage form. In the first cell, then, 56 per cent (1.67/3.00) of nominations are represented. The bottom row presents the identical analysis for those nominated low on leadership. Here, as might be anticipated, the trend of mean size is reversed, reflecting the high correlation between leadership and followership.

TABLE 3

Mean assignment of leadership and followership nominations for the three friends nominated

$$(N = 186)$$

	High	Not mentioned	Low	Sum of means
Leadership nominations of three friends	$M = .83$ $\sigma = .81$	$M = 2.11$ $\sigma = .71$	$M = .06$ $\sigma = .24$	3.00
Followership nominations of three friends	$M = 1.33$ $\sigma = .73$	$M = 1.63$ $\sigma = .73$	$M = .04$ $\sigma = .18$	3.00

An analysis similar to the previous one is presented in Table 3. The focus of attention here is on the disposition of friends within leadership and followership nomination categories. Specifically, consideration has been given to the mean number of the nominators' friends who are nominated, on the average, as high or low or not at all on leadership, in the top row, and on followership, in the bottom row. From the first two top cells it will be noted that, of the three friends, an average of .83 of them are nominated high on leadership whereas 2.11 of them are disregarded in these nominations. This stands in contrast to the adjacent bottom cells where means of 1.33 and 1.63 friends are nominated high on followership or disregarded. These means, of course, may be simply transformed to percentages as indicated for Table 2. This over-all pattern is noteworthy in demonstrating that an average of more than two out of three friends are *disregarded* on leadership nominations; so far as followership nominations are concerned, no such marked tendency evidences itself. Significant t values ($p < .001$) were obtained for the first and second columns.

Discussion

With respect to the fundamental questions underlying this investigation the results indicate first that leadership and followership nominations are intimately related in a positive direction. The implication of this finding is that the more desired followers tend to be at the upper extremes of the leadership distribution; a corollary of this would be that those who are low or disregarded on leadership nominations are not viewed as desirable followers.

The second major finding is that leadership and followership nominations are, to a considerable extent, independent of the friendship choice of the nominators. This finding tends to substantiate the fact that peer nominations are not mere "popularity contests," but represent, at least for the variables of this study, evaluations of the individual's potential for performance largely independent of the dimension of friendship.

In discussion of the relatively high correspondence between leadership and followership, the crux of the matter lies, of course, in our definition of followership. The term may be broadly approached from the viewpoint of the leader or that of the led, i.e. the followers. In other words, the followers may be evaluated on their capacity as followers or their willingness to be followers. One may adopt either or both views. We have chosen to view follower-ship as it is judged from the leadership standpoint. We have made this choice for two reasons: first, the reality of institutional de-mands, and, second, the nature of the sociometric process and its established validity. A composite of followership nominations from potential leaders—followership as viewed by all group members acting as a leader—presents a reasonably satisfactory picture of this kind of followership. As it emerges here, then, our definition of followership is the extent to which an individual is desired by po-tential leaders of a group functioning within a circumscribed insti-tutional context.

In keeping with this line of thinking, an additional analysis was conducted to determine whether individuals chosen high on lead-ership differed essentially in their choice of followers from indi-viduals chosen low on leadership. By correlating the followership scores derived from nominations made by individuals in the top half of the leadership continuum with followership scores derived from nominations made by individuals in the lower half, it was found that the leadership status factor made little difference in the selection of followers; the correlation between the followership scores obtained independently from these two nominator groups was .82. Noting that the split-half reliability is a correlation be-tween two sets of followership scores obtained independently of the leadership status of those making nominations, we find this r of .82 accords well with followership's uncorrected reliability of .83.

The finding that good leaders are also judged as good followers makes sense when viewed within an institutional framework like the military establishment. The principle represented applies as well to other institutions, however. With the increasing complexity of our society, the role of the institutional leader demands some-thing more than leaping on a white charger to gallop off in a solely self-determined direction. Typically, he must effectively lead his group in directions which have been assigned to that group. Given this circumstance, the leader must himself be a good follower or his group may find itself destroyed or performing inefficiently in a total organizational mission. This point has been well elucidated in a number of studies, among them an industrial study of the first-line supervisor by Pelz (1952), discussed in Chapter 3.

It seems reasonable from the findings that one cannot make the simple assumption that those individuals not chosen as leaders may be integrated within the group as effective followers. Then, too, re-enforcement has been offered the view that friendship is not necessarily crucial to other forms of group status. As with all such studies, however, generalizations from particular samples should be handled with caution. On the other hand, generalizations to the military institution—from which this sample was drawn—may be reasonably made. Finally, while no pretense has been made here that any broad implications for sociometry have been contributed, it is hoped that, within an applied sphere, certain fundamental notions regarding the interrelationship of leadership, followership, and friendship may have been developed.

Summary and conclusions

The relationship between leadership, followership, and friendship peer nominations was studied within eight sections of Naval Aviation Cadets, N = 187. Two related problems of some significance to the interpretation of peer-nomination data were specified: (a) a consideration of followership status as an element of leadership status; and (b) an examination of friendship as a variable underlying leadership and/or followership nominations. The results indicated that leadership and followership nominations were related to a high degree, $r = .92$. Friendship nominations were *not* found to bear appreciably on this relationship, $r_{LF.Fr} = .90$. Leadership and friendship were found to be correlated at a significantly *lower* level than followership and friendship. An average of more than two out of three friendship nominees were not mentioned at all in the leadership nominations. Finally, the leadership status of nominators, as determined from peer nominations, was found to be unrelated to the followership choices which they made.

From the results it may be concluded that peer nominations on leadership are by no means a total function of friendship ties; quite the contrary, friendship appears to play only a minor role in the emergence of leadership nominations. Furthermore, followership status is not necessarily implied by nonleader status on peer nominations. It appears evident that the popular dichotomy between leadership and followership is in need of reappraisal. Rather understandably, the nature of our complex, hierarchical institutions demands that the effective leader be equally effective as a follower. It may be considerably more realistic, therefore, to consider characteristics of followership as one functional component of good leadership.

7

Group consensus and group attraction

One of the reasons for an interest in interpersonal perception is the fact that directly or indirectly it bears upon group attractiveness, and ultimately effectiveness. By now, a substantial literature has accumulated which suggests that this is the case. Homans (1950), for example, contends that interaction between people may yield a friendliness which in turn smoothes the way for cooperative enterprise. The work of Newcomb (1956) affords similar implications, where there exists a shared frame of reference.

Despite problems of measurement and conceptualization (cf. Steiner, 1955; Cronbach, 1958), the weight of evidence suggests two intertwined statements of probability: similarity of view, a common frame of reference, some mutually-held attitudes, yield greater group attraction; but, too, the attractiveness of a group to members leads to greater consensus among them (cf. Festinger, 1950).

Adapted from a paper prepared originally as *Technical Report No. VI* under Office of Naval Research Contract 1849(00) with the Carnegie Institute of Technology, April 1959.

Problem

In this research we shall be exploring the relationship between attraction of a group to its members, determined by member responses to a questionnaire, with several discrepancy scores and concordance measures derived from a values list administered at three sequential stages. The prediction is that greater group attraction is positively related to greater group consensus and that this may be discerned as a developing phenomenon over time.

Subjects and procedure

The sample consisted of eight sections of officer candidates in training at the Naval OCS in Newport, Rhode Island. Sections numbered approximately 30 each; random assignment insured comparability of one to the other.

The program at the OCS is of sixteen weeks' duration, with an orientation week introduced before the actual onset of the training cycle. During this one-week period, student personnel are assigned to sections, receive books and clothing, take classification tests, and are given orientation lectures, but do not attend formal classes as such.

All of the subjects were recent graduates of college who had volunteered for this training. The mean age for this group was 22 years with only a minimal dispersion above this figure.

During the orientation week, after the sections had been together for just several days, and twice more at intervals of three weeks apart, subjects were asked to rank the following list of ten value statements in order of importance to them:

1. Having a good social standing and the right kind of people as friends.
2. Having good looks and appearance, good build, height, etc
3. Being sure of a steady income, with good living conditions
4. Having a good religious understanding and faith.

5. Being liked and respected and feeling you "belong."
6. Being in good physical and mental health.
7. Having a chance to develop some special talent, interest or hobby.
8. Having a good ability to understand things, a good education and general information.
9. Being satisfied in relationships with members of the opposite sex.
10. Being satisfied with your work or job.

Following this, in each instance, subjects were instructed to go over this same list, presented on a separate form, and estimate the way in which their section as a whole would rank these.

For each section it was possible to determine a "norm" based upon the relative ranks yielded by summing those assigned by section members. Using this norm as a base, the Cronbach-Gleser "D" (1953) was then calculated by squaring each deviation from the norm, summing these, and taking its square root. This was done both for the self-rankings (S) and for the estimate-rankings (EST), at all three stages.

By comparing a subject's own ranking of values with his estimate-rankings, still another discrepancy score was derived, i.e. S-EST, at each time. The particular utility of this score resides in its indication of an individual's perceived difference between himself and the members of his section.

Finally, a questionnaire was presented to the subjects at the same time as the final administration with one item especially centered on determining the attractiveness of the section to individuals alone and collectively. That item read as follows: "If you were going to sea right now, how important would it be for you to be assigned with the men in your own section?" The alternatives for response were as follows:

1. Would want very much to go with the men in my section.
2. Would probably prefer to go with the men in my section.
3. Wouldn't matter one way or the other.

4. Would not want to go with the men in my section.
5. Undecided.

Table 1 presents the response pattern for this question in terms of frequency for each of the eight sections. As a rough gauge of section differences from high to low, a mean response was calculated as the basis for ranking the sections.

TABLE 1

Frequency of response by category to questionnaire item on continued affiliation with section for the eight sections of the sample

Section	N	Mean response	Rank for attraction	Category				
				(1)	(2)	(3)	(4)	(5)
D	29	2.13	1	7	12	9	1	0
H	32	2.19	2	7	12	13	0	0
A	31	2.23	3	6	13	9	2	1
E	32	2.25	4	4	16	11	0	1
G	27	2.39	5	3	7	17	0	0
F	31	2.45	6	3	13	13	2	0
B	30	2.55	7	2	9	17	1	1
C	28	2.61	8	1	9	17	1	0
$N = 240$			Sum	33	91	106	7	3

$\chi^2 = 14.15$; df = 7 (Columns 1 and 2 vs. 3 and 4); $P < .05$

It will be noted that 106 of the 240 subjects responded "3" indicating an indifference on this issue. Taking account of the variant frequencies overall, an equalizing split was made between those who answered in a positive way by a "1" or "2" ($N = 124$) as against those not giving a positive response by their "3" or "4" answer ($N = 113$). Omitting the three cases answering "Undecided," a two-by-eight chi-square indicated a difference between sections on this attraction measure significant at the 5% level.

Analyses and results

In Table 2, ranks for section attraction are related to ranks for the S, EST, and S-EST discrepancy scores over time. The means obtained for the section as a whole on these three measures were ranked from 1 to 8, going from low discrepancy to high discrepancy. An overall mean for the three readings of each of the three scores was computed and is presented as a basis for yielding an overall rank for the measure. Rhos are given for each discrepancy score rank with the section's rank for attraction. Since eight items are ranked, the standard error of Rho is equal to .36 which means that a Rho of .72 is required for the 5% level of significance.

TABLE 2

Rank order correlations (Rho) for three discrepancy scores with mean section attraction at three points in training

Discrepancy scores	Time in training			
	Orientation week	Third week	Sixth week	Overall
Self from norm (S)	.12	.47	.39	.43
Estimate from norm (EST)	.20	−.13	−.02	−.05
Self from estimate (S-EST)	.60	.23	.74 *	.62

* 5% level

In this table, the 5% level for Rho was obtained only for the comparison of S-EST with rank for attraction at the sixth week. The value is .74 which is significant and may be interpreted to indicate that *to the extent that members of a section perceive other members of the section to be similar to themselves, the attraction of the section is higher.* Thus, a greater disparity between self-ranking and estimate-ranking should reflect a lower level of group attraction. The other Rhos for this variable are not as high but are in the same range in two instances and indicative of a trend.

This analysis was extended into data appearing in Table 3. For this we turned to the raw ranking data, quite apart from any considerations of deviations from a norm, in order to measure section consensus directly. A rank concordance of response for the eight sections was determined by making use of the Kendall "W" for the self-rankings of the values list and the estimate-rankings of the values list, at three stages.

TABLE 3

Rank order correlations (Rho) with mean section attraction for magnitude of Kendall "W" for two rankings at three points in training

| Rankings | Time in training | | | Overall |
	Orientation week	Third week	Sixth week	
Self	.10	.41	.43	.41
Estimate	−.22	−.12	.10	−.14

Here again, Rhos were computed between the section's rank for W, where the higher value is indicative of greater consensus, and the section's rank for attraction. Most revealing of the finding here is the difference between the consistently rising positive value for the self-ranking data, and the low-level, but negatively related trends evidenced by the Rhos for the estimate rankings. The Rho for overall ranks for self-ranking with the overall rank for estimate ranking was .29. The implication of this clustering of findings is that a similarity among section members in their *personal* ranking of these values is more closely tied in with the section's attraction than is their correspondence when it comes to making estimate. This would appear to signify, among other possibilities, that the way they are rather than the way they perceive themselves to be bears more directly upon the attraction of these sections to their members.

The effect of group attraction on the interrelation of sociometric continua was still another feature examined within these section.

It was reasonable to expect that the mean number of friends named "high" on leadership might be revealing in this regard. Since five friends and five high leadership nominees were required, this value could vary from 0 to 5.00. A presentation of the methodology utilized in the sociometric phase of this study will be found in Chapters 10, 11, and 12.

For the top four ranking sections on attraction, the mean number of friends thus nominated over three times, was 2.20; for the bottom four sections, the figure was 2.01. This betrayed a trend in the hypothesized direction, but an analysis of variance for high vs. low attraction yielded an F that was not significant; the effect of time, however, was significant at the 5% level ($F = 5.59$; $N = 18$); the first administration of these sociometric forms (during orientation week) yielded a mean of 2.33, and the last administration (during the sixth week of training) one of 2.03; the intermediate (third week) mean was 1.95. Thus, the general pattern of a lower relationship between these variables over time was significant, but the tendency for a higher relationship between these in sections of high attraction was not. The interaction effect here, it should be added, was nonsignificant.

Discussion

This study has examined the relationship between certain indices of consensus and the attraction of a group to its members. In view of the small number of groups involved, and the consequent necessity to have very high relationships to achieve anything near significance, several of the findings are more in the nature of trends than confirmed hypotheses. The data do lead, however, to essential support of the view that perceived consensus, in terms of value orientations, is positively related to group attraction.

In the functional group sense, military training sections are limited in scope; hence these findings should be interpreted in that light. The only relationship that reached significance was that between members' perception of their section as being like themselves, on the ordering of values, and their willingness to remain in it later. This result might require scrutiny in terms of the relatively large number of trainees in all who were indifferent to this latter course.

It is of course entirely understandable that there should be only a limited involvement in section identity, or "attraction," precisely because of the limited quality of such sustaining *group* attributes as a common group goal and volition in membership, and because of the presence of intermember competition for standing. The basis for group attraction in these sections would more likely reside in friendship ties of the "psyche-group" sort rather than in "sociogroup" ties growing out of the pursuit of a mutual task, as is more the case with a ship's crew. These characteristics make "classes" of this sort different qualitatively from groups functioning in the field. Yet, granting this restriction, it is all the more noteworthy that the major consideration prompting this research should have been sustained.

Summary

From research with eight training sections of naval officer candidates, numbering about 30 each, data are presented on the relationship of group attraction to various measures of group consensus. A notably high correspondence was found between the rank order of attraction these sections had for members and ranks based on the smallness of disparity between members' own ranking of a values list and their estimate of the section's ranking. Group consensus in the self-ranking of the values list, as measured by the Kendall "W," was consistently but not significantly related over time to the section's rank for attraction to members.

III

Sociometric methods of assessment

In this section we present several studies with a method of assessment growing out of sociometry and known as the peer-nomination technique. Fundamentally this involves a procedure for evaluation through pooled co-worker judgments. Particularly within the armed forces, the use of such evaluations as an integral part of personnel research programs has been widespread.

Prior research on the peer-nomination technique, affording extensive evidence in support of its essential validity and reliability, is presented in Chapter Eight. In this vein, a study of leadership nominations as predictors of success in flight training provides additional evidence in Chapter Nine.

Some of the questions concerning the utility of the technique are dealt with by the research presented in Chapters Ten, Eleven, and Twelve. Of special relevance are the matters of reliability of ratings, the validity of ratings given at an early point in interpersonal contact, and the issue of whether considerations of friendship bear upon both of these. Research on the use of peer nominations as a method of morale assessment, and a comparison of its utility with other devices are presented in Chapter Thirteen.

8

An introduction to the peer-nomination technique

For more than two decades, research has been pursued with a method of evaluation known as the "peer rating." Its form is quite simple, which fact both accounts for its ready application, and a possible failure to comprehend its power as a psychological tool when employed with discernment. Indeed, because of its very simplicity the peer rating can readily be misused with poor consequences. In this chapter, we intend to provide a review of appropriate uses of the technique which have yielded noteworthy findings.

Basically, a "peer rating" involves each group member's assessment of every other group member on a recognizable quality, some examples being effectiveness on a task, popularity, and leadership. From these ratings, a composite score is obtained which can be used to predict a criterion, or serve itself as a criterion against which other factors are validated. There are two essential variations of this process. In one, each group member literally *ranks* the others through the assignment of a score or by an actual process of ranking. In the second, each individual *nominates* a specified number of his fellows whom he considers "high" or "low" on the

Adapted in part from an address prepared for the XIII International Congress of Applied Psychology at Rome, April 1958, and subsequently published in French in the journal *Revue de Psychologie Appliquée*, 1958, 8, 189-198.

quality being measured. This survey emphasizes the major work undertaken with this second approach—the peer nomination.

The peer nomination as a psychological instrument

Interpersonal ratings are surely not new to psychology, although for evaluation they usually tend to take two forms: ratings by superiors on subordinates, or ratings by external observers, i.e. by personnel interviewers, or clinicians. In the peer rating, we in effect extend evaluation to take in more raters: those who are in close contact with one another on an equal basis. This has virtue in several ways because it takes account of the reality of everyday life. Those who work side by side, or who are in training together, are in a better position to observe each other in a natural environment; the artificiality or atypicality of behavior often produced by status differentials is removed; and a larger pool of evaluators is afforded, thus setting the ground for an increased reliability of rating.

Since any form of peer rating is an evaluation made *by* and *among* those who occupy comparable status and who have a consistency of interaction over time, the definition of who qualifies as a "peer" is clearly of more than casual interest. It is presupposed that members of the group are familiar with one another as a central consideration for the validity of their appraisals. Given this condition, the most common rating form is the peer nomination.

The popularity of the nomination device rests fundamentally upon the ease with which it is understood and responded to by raters. Consider the alternatives of total ranking or scaled judgments, person-by-person. For several reasons, both the ranking or scaling procedures prove to be somewhat less manageable in administration. For example, ranking all the members of a group of twenty people proves a burden, even to the trained observer—and the greatest difficulty is likely to be encountered in the middle range. In fact, precisely this consideration has led to a recognition that it is really the top and bottom cases on a distribution which need be identified in order to establish a metric. The peer nomination does precisely that. It requests of the rater that he name some specified number of those who fall at the extremes of a continuum he perceives to exist for a characteristic like leadership, work competence, dependability, or what you will.

While an extension, therefore, of more traditional psychological rating methods, it will also be seen that the peer nomination bears a family resemblance to a form of sociometry. But there are differences involved of content, or intent, as well as of procedure. In the pure sociometric case as conceived by Moreno, the aim is to discern the choice pattern of a group, that is to say, its internal links of attraction and repulsion among members (cf. Criswell, 1943). This is facilitated by the sociogram as a graphic representation of these. Quite apart from this concern, however, the peer nomination is designed to array individuals in terms of a consistent measure of some observable personal characteristic. Whatever similarities between the traditional sociogram as a focus of study and the peer nomination, the significant distinguishing feature lies in how data are subsequently treated, and toward what end. This leads appropriately now to the matter of scoring.

Scoring

In scoring the peer nomination, a number of approaches may be followed, the most straightforward being a simple sum of nominations received by an individual, both plus and minus. One may take a further step and expand this procedure to include an index of rank; thus, weights may be assigned where, if there are to be five high and five low nominees required, the highest nominee of each nominator's five top nominees would receive a weight of $+5$, the next highest a $+4$, and so on; the bottom nominees would receive corresponding weights of -5, -4, and so on, in the same fashion. This procedure discerns ranks within nominations, though its virtue has not been demonstrated absolutely. In general, the simple sum may suffice quite adequately (e.g. Kubany, 1957).

A very sophisticated methodology has been employed by Katz (1953) who takes account of the status among his peers of the nominator in weighting his nominations. Gardner and Thompson (1956) employ a procedure to obtain nominations, in the first place, on a scale with an absolute frame of reference, e.g. "among all men you have known."

Experience has shown that peer nominations tend to be highly reliable, and the specifics of this finding will be set forth below. This is a function of the fact that one rarely finds a person who has received an opposing number of both plus and minus nominations. Therefore, it is most usual and to be expected that the scores derived should be distributed in a substantially normal fashion from a high plus value through zero, to a high minus value. With this raw distribution in hand, it is possible to develop standard scores reflecting placement in the group from a mean of zero, or some such similar conversion procedure to remove sign.

Kinds of dimensions

The most widespread initial use of the peer nomination for personnel assessment occurred in the Armed Forces during World War II. The large array of studies conducted with this instrument frequently involved officer candidates in training and accordingly a great focus of attention was understandably on leadership. More recently, other characteristics have been treated in military research, thus broadening it considerably to include factors such as motivation and probability of success, both in training as well as in the role of an officer.

In civilian settings, too, work has proceeded with peer nominations of various characteristics. Many experimental studies of small groups in social psychology employ nominations on characteristics of perceived performance as part of their procedure. In a validity study of the behavioral correlates of the California Authoritarianism Scale (F Scale), peer nominations were used to secure criterion measures (Titus, 1957). An intensive investigation of the relevant attributes of outstanding medical students by Kubany (1957) included ten dimensions of peer nominations. This sampling of illustrations simply suggests the multiple possibilities for assessing characteristics, even of personality, through peer nominations. The more impressive are the data on validity and reliability of this instrument to which we turn now.

Regarding validity and reliability

When considering the value of any measurement device, two questions immediately arise: Is the device valid? And is it reliable? A substantial literature has been accumulated on the validity and reliability of peer nominations. From this work, one significant fact emerges repeatedly: peer nominations represent a more superior, consistent predictor of performance criteria across situations than any other single variable. The evidence, mainly from military studies, is quite clear on this point (Hollander, 1954b).

Perhaps the first substantial work with the peer-nomination technique, so far as personnel research is concerned, was done in the navy, in a study of aviation squadrons. From this project came evidence of the utility of this method of evaluation in pinpointing the qualities making for the "wanted" pilot, as opposed to the "unwanted" pilot. This has been documented in a comprehensive article by Jenkins (1948).

Within this same era, Williams and Leavitt (1947), two navy psychologists at the Marine Corps Officer Candidate School, were utilizing such ratings with officer candidates to predict their field performance in combat. Their results were particularly striking. They found that "...sociometric group opinion was a more valid predictor both of success in Officer Candidate School and of combat performance than several objective tests..." (p. 291). Furthermore, peer ratings were significantly better than superiors' ratings in predicting the criteria. They conclude that peer evaluation has greater validity than these other measures because group members have more time to observe each other than do the superior officers, they know each other in a realistic context and react more directly to each other's social behavior. These are all conditions, they observe, which are favorable to "informed judgments" (p. 291).

In a definitive study done at the Signal Corps OCS, Wherry and Fryer (1949) found support for the higher validity of peer nominations against superior ratings, in predicting leadership performance. These, they contend, "appear to be the purest measure of 'leadership' . . . Nominations by class appear to be better measures of the leadership factor than any other variable" (p. 157). With this evidence at hand, they reject the argument that these ratings are mainly a contest for popularity rather than a valid criterion. Additional support for their position is considered especially in Chapters 6 and 12 in this work.

Confirmation of these results has come also from extensive follow-up studies of graduates of the West Point Military Academy (1948, 1949). In this research, nominations by peers made at the Academy were found to be a significant predictor of performance as an officer after several years in the field. Furthermore, in a study of pilot trainees in the navy (see Chapter 9), peer nominations on leadership before flight training yielded a significant validity coefficient in the prediction of the pass-fail criterion in the flight phase. The fact that leadership nominations *can* predict such a complex criterion as successful completion of flight training some 14 months later raises enthusiasm for the potentialities of the technique.

At this point, one may properly begin to raise a query concerning the composition of peer evaluations. What are the kinds of considerations which go to make up these ratings in the first place? A peer nomination was used for a time at the navy's Pre-Flight School at Pensacola asking for reasons *why* cadets nominated peers "high" or "low" on leadership. This had been tried previously with some success by Jenkins (1948) and his colleagues. Drawing on these data, Richardson, Bellows, and Henry (1951) developed a forced-choice rating form which embodied descriptive phrases ac-

tually used by the cadets. Two interchangeable forms were ultimately designed; they report that when these forms are completed
on a cadet by two classmates chosen at random, the forms correlate with the peer-nomination criterion at the .76 and .77 levels
respectively (p. 19).

Another kind of answer to this has been provided to some degree
by the research done by Tupes, Borg, and Friedman (1953) in the
Air Force. In their study, they factor-analyzed data drawn from
OCS peer ratings of the "paired comparison" variety. Effectively,
this modification requires each candidate to evaluate each of his
fellow flight members on some 30 specific areas of behavior plus
evaluation on a general proficiency variable. From the analyses, six
factors were obtained which, after rotation to orthogonal simple
structure, appeared as one general factor, four group factors, and
one residual factor. The group factors are described as: administrative ability, working effectively with others, striving to do a good
job, and acceptance of organizational responsibility (p. 6). Notice
how these can account for effective interpersonal qualities, personal involvement with a task, and assimilation to organizational
structure and goals. The authors conclude that ". . . OCS candidates, although not able to discriminate satisfactorily among the
30 specific behaviors . . . do consider several different variables
when evaluating each other" (p. 7).

In addition to providing independent validity, scores derived
from peer nominations have been found to be highly reliable as
well. Just as with other measures, two major approaches may be
followed in determining the reliability of these scores. One may
deal with the internal consistency of the nominations made within
a given group at a set point in time; or, alternatively, one may view
their stability over time as reflected in repeat administrations. Both
procedures are in current use.

The calculation of single-stage reliability, i.e. internal consistency, is accomplished by splitting the raters on an odd-even basis
and then computing two measures of status for each individual,
one from each of the two sub-groups thus provided. The correla·

tion between these two measures is then treated by the Spearman-Brown formula to yield a corrected reliability coefficient. Applying this method to groups of Naval Aviation Cadets, the writer has found coefficients for peer nominations on leadership to be quite routinely between .85 and .90 (Hollander, 1954b). Additional research indicates comparable results.

The bulk of the studies already reported find a high degree of stability of the peer-nomination score over time. As an example, Wherry and Fryer (1949) indicate that "... the reliability of nominations after four months is outstandingly higher than that of the other variables upon which the test was made. This is probably further evidence of the fact that the nominating technique has the property of early identification of the members of the group who constitute the two extremes of the leadership distribution" (p. 159). Other work supports this assertion.

From a study with trainees in the Marine Corps Officer Screening Course, Anderhalter, *et al.* (1952) report an average reliability of .71 from ratings made during the first and third weeks. Whatever the method of determination applied, then, the relatively high reliability of peer-nomination scores appears to persist.

Some newer findings

Though it has been established that the peer-nomination procedure affords adequate validity and reliability, it is nevertheless true that several questions remain to be answered for optimum utilization. One of the most persistent of these concerns the issue of variations in both reliability and validity which may be attributable to the nature of the *quality* on which the nominator is instructed to make his nominations. Related to this is the dual consideration of the *time* and *context* of the evaluations.

We have approached these issues by administering various peer-nomination forms to 23 groups of officer students, numbering 30 each, at the Newport Naval OCS. The reports of this work appear in Chapters 10, 11, and 12. Four forms were utilized. They dealt with leadership, motivation for naval service, probable success in training, and success as a future officer. All forms were administered at least three times during the training period of sixteen weeks' duration.

Reliability was calculated for each form, at each time of administration. For split-half reliability, the earliest nominations, made after four or five days of contact, yielded scores having corrected reliabilities of about .90. Though some minor rise in this value was discerned for scores obtained from later nominations, the increase was not appreciable or significant. Furthermore, a high intercorrelation of scores from the same form, administered at different times, was also found. Thus, the internal consistency of the scores was high throughout the sequence of administrations, and scores from even the earliest stage of training showed a high correspondence with the later scores. The score for leadership evidenced the highest intercorrelation with itself over time, being about .87.

Validity was initially determined from criteria accessible in the training program, i.e. pass-fail, final academic average, and final military aptitude grade, assigned by superiors. For these criteria the peer-nomination scores gave significant, and differentially discriminating, validity coefficients. As an example, nominations for probability of success in the school, secured even before the onset of formal classes, were significantly correlated with the ultimate pass-fail and academic criteria. In general, nominations obtained very early in training, and certainly by the third week, provided completely comparable validity to that of the later nominations. As will be seen in Chapter 11, a follow-up study of the validity of these nominations in predicting fleet performance provides further confirmation in this vein. Data were obtained from fitness report ratings given by their senior officers to 629 of the original officer candidates from Newport, after they had had an average of three years of duty as officers. Such ratings are given no less than once every six months as a routine procedure. Scores from nominations for performance as a "future officer" correlated .40 with this criterion, beginning with those from the third week of training and not exceeding this level for the sixth and twelfth week nomination scores; a value of .24 was obtained even for the first nomination, before the onset of training. The only predictor from OCS achieving a degree of validity near the third week nomination score was final academic average with a coefficient of .41 against this same criterion. Early nominations therefore sustain prediction of later performance when properly focused at the outset.

In the original Newport study we also probed the relationship of nominations to friendship ties, since it is sometimes argued that peer nominations are contaminated by a friendship factor. As reported in Chapter 12, our data do not support this contention. Fewer than half of a nominator's acknowledged friends were nominated by him as being high on other characteristics. If anything, the data suggest that friendship ties are a function of status ascription, rather than the reverse. Moreover, there is no basis either for the belief that friendship, in the aggregative sense of "popularity," limits the validity of peer-nomination scores for other characteristics.

Implications and applications

The evidence supporting the validity and reliability of the peer ratings technique is consistent and substantial. Nominations *do* predict diverse behavioral phenomena reliably. But this stands as a mere beginning. It will be apparent that the potential inherent in the technique has yet to be seen in its fuller aspects.

Viewed broadly, the implication of the work already completed is that group opinion, taken as a composite, may yield information about an individual which is not being tapped at present by other measures. The very core of the matter, as has been suggested by Williams and Leavitt (1947), is that such group evaluations are based upon "informed judgments" drawn from personal interactions. This suggests that still other qualities may be measured through peer nominations and that advances into the general field of psychological assessment may be made.

It can be argued, of course, that broader extensions might not be appropriate since the evidence reported stems so much from military training programs. This is not so crucial, however, since the nomination technique rests not on situational considerations as much as it does on the stability of the group and its potential for inter-member contact. Thus, a group of industrial trainees could readily be assessed by this method, so long as they had been together for some minimal period of time. A variety of relevant criteria can be predicted with such groups, though reports on applications of this kind are not so readily found in the professional literature.

Another often expressed concern is whether group members might not resent rating one another. Our experience indicates that though they may, they need not. This depends, of course, on the way in which the task is presented. Many times we have found excellent cooperation from subjects if several guidelines were followed. Among them are: a clear rationale for the ratings is presented initially; the point is firmly made that these evaluations are pooled so that no *one* individual's rating of another is critical; and group members are seated apart, preferably in columns, so that they cannot see each other's paper.

So long as members of a group have been interacting together, it is feasible to consider the use of a peer nomination where the assessment of some manifest characteristic is desired. The appropriateness of this in military officer training is clear; prompt identification of marginal trainees saves not only time and money, but human effort and later disappointment as well. However, this is equally true of a multitude of nonmilitary situations. For instance, it is not unreasonable to think that management might make use of peer nominations to assist in the process of personnel promotion. Admittedly, this requires some degree of subtlety on the part of administrators lest employees gain the erroneous impression that this constitutes the *sole* standard of evaluation. Nonetheless, the selection of personnel for key jobs may be considerably facilitated through the availability of information relative to their co-workers' view of them. Doubtless, some will raise the objection that this procedure puts a kind of administrative decision in the hands of subordinates. But that is precisely the point: information from nominations is more than a simple tabulation of votes—it predicts criteria; and it bears directly on organizational goals of optimum performance and effectiveness. Van Zelst (1952), for example, has reported that the selection of work teams by application of a peer nomination, to maximize workers' choice of co-workers, leads to increased productivity.

Possible applications to problems of morale are equally promising, as is pointed out in Chapter 13. It is entirely feasible that an index of morale for employee units could be gleaned through the implementation of a nomination form specifying "interest in the job," or some similar characteristic. One complication is the possible unwillingness of employees to make such ratings if it were felt that *individual scores* would be reported to management. Such a situation could be obviated, however, by having the data gathered by an agency external to the organization which would report only group scores to the administrative level.

Along the same line, measures of group cohesiveness—another approach to morale—can be elicited from peer data. The extent to which individuals in a group are "underchosen" or "underranked" affords a useful index of this group characteristic (cf. Proctor & Loomis, 1951). It has long since been observed that morale is closely bound up with the cohesiveness, or solidarity of a group. And this is the kind of information which is most readily obtainable from applications of this technique.

Still another addition to the basic peer ratings method is offered by Anderhalter, *et al.* (1952). In their work they have evolved an index which reflects the degree to which group members, either individually or collectively, are accurate in ranking each other. Put simply, this procedure compares the rankings made by each individual with the rankings from the pooled judgment of the group. Where the average index for the group is small, group members have a superior awareness of how the others "stack up" on the quality being measured. Where the index is large, group members are inaccurate in their appraisal of the status of others on this quality. In a sense, then, this procedure also serves as a method for indexing group cohesiveness or solidarity.

A related method of extracting supplementary data from peer nominations has been studied at Pensacola. The procedure used is to request each individual to give his own self-rank on leadership, and then an estimate of the actual leadership rank he will secure from the pooled judgments of the group. This is directly incorporated into the leadership nomination form. Discrepancy scores from the actual group rank are then derived for each of these two "personal ranks." These scores, in turn, can be related to the basic nomination score or some other criterion. Another exploration of this method has been reported also in a study done in the Air Force (Flyer, *et al.*, 1953).

The applications cited represent merely a sampling within a range of potentialities. Quite obviously, however, the peer-nomination technique is not suited to every evaluation problem, though it has distinctive utility as a supplemental measure. And that is the central point. Peer nominations have multiple applications as a device enhancing psychological prediction and the study of interpersonal processes.

9

Peer nominations on leadership as a predictor of the pass-fail criterion in naval air training

As reported in Chapter 8, studies by Williams and Leavitt (1947) at the Marine Corps Officer Candidate School, by Wherry and Fryer (1949) at the Signal Corps Officer Candidate School, and by McClure, Tupes, and Dailey (1951) at the Air Force Officer Candidate School have lent substantiation to the validity of peer nominations on leadership against various performance and operational criteria.

While this evidence is clear-cut, the criteria utilized for validation have quite properly tended to be directly related to the initial character of the nomination. It has been assumed, with good reason, that peer nominations on leadership should be expected to correlate with a criterion derived from some variety of leadership behavior or performance measure. On the other hand, there exist very little research regarding the applicability of peer nomination *on leadership* to performance or operational criteria presumably unrelated to leadership behavior. It may well be that the so-called

Adapted from the *Journal of Applied Psychology*, 1954, 38, 150-153, with permission of the publisher, the American Psychological Association.

"leadership nominations" identify characteristics of the individual which relate to criteria in the spheres of cognition, or personal adjustment, or such a complex as ability to solo an aircraft successfully. With this prospect in view, the current investigation explored a fundamental relationship, that is, peer nominations on leadership, during pre-flight school, and success or failure through the whole of flight training. Fundamentally, two questions were posed: Do peer nominations on leadership during pre-flight correlate significantly with a pass-fail criterion for the entire flight training program? And, if so, how well do these nominations predict this criterion compared to other variables from the same stage of training, i.e. pre-flight?

Procedure

A total of 268 Naval Aviation Cadets who entered pre-flight training during late 1951 were taken as a study sample. This group consisted of nine consecutively formed "sections" of about thirty cadets each. The cadets had already been preselected for the training program on criteria of physical fitness, age, minimum educational level, intelligence, mechanical aptitude, and background characteristics.

At the end of their third month of pre-flight training, each section was administered a leadership nomination form which presented the individual cadet with a list of his sectionmates from which he was asked to nominate the three men from the list *best* qualified for the hypothetical position of "student commander" and the three men *least* qualified. Furthermore, the instructions specifically stated that the nominator was to evaluate his nominees with regard to their "present and eventual success as military leaders." In this way, it was anticipated that confusion regarding the "leadership standard" to be applied would be obviated. It should be noted, too, that cadets were directed to ignore athletic ability as a factor in their nominations. This was considered to be a necessary and desirable part of the set in order to place some control on an ability which seemed likely to be closely related to physique. Nominations were weighted $+3$ for "highest," $+2$ for second "highest," and $+1$ for third "highest"; similarly, weights of -3, -2 and -1 were assigned for the three corresponding "low" categories. A summation of these weights for each cadet was then taken as his leadership nomination score. The distribution of such scores yielded a unimodal and approximately symmetrical distribution. A standard score transformation was then utilized to afford a comparable index of the cadet's relative standing on leadership *within his own section*.[1]

In addition to this leadership score (LDR) derived from peer nominations, a number of other measures on the cadets were available from pre-flight. These were: ACE (College Level) Test scores obtained during the cadet's first week in training; Officer-Like-Qualities score (OLQ) assigned at the end of pre-flight by the officers in command to evaluate the cadet on qualities of leadership, military bearing, discipline and the like; and final pre-flight average (FAV) based upon performance in all courses.[2]

After a period of some eighteen months had elapsed, a follow-up of the study sample revealed that of the 268 cadets involved, 179 had passed flight training and had received their wings, 32 had failed flight training, 28 had withdrawn from training voluntarily, and the balance of 29 cadets had been separated from the training program as a result of physical disqualification, illness, violation of contract, or some similar reason. With criterion groups thus established, a matrix of intercorrelations among the predictor variables was constructed and biserial r's were computed for each of these variables against the pass-fail criterion.

[1] This technique derives substantially from one developed as part of ONR Contract No. N onr-o-3400 by Richardson, Bellows, Henry, and Company.
[2] It should be noted that at no time were scores achieved by cadets on peer nominations available to authorities in the Training Command who assign OLQ or performance grades to cadets. Moreover, the cadets themselves did not know the ACE scores, final grades, or OLQ grades of their sectionmates at the time they made their nominations on leadership.

Findings

Table 1 presents the matrix of intercorrelations, validity coefficients, and beta weights for the four predictor variables. Among these, it is apparent that final pre-flight average (FAV) predicts the pass-fail criterion at the highest relative level and with the greatest weight. This tends to reinforce the finding of a validity study of pre-flight grades (Hollander, 1952). Second to final average, however, is the leadership score (LDR) which the cadet received from the nominations made by his sectionmates *before* he entered the flight phase of training, and *well over a year prior to the time he might receive his wings*. It should be noted, too, that the magnitude of the difference between the validity coefficients for FAV and LDR may readily be ascribed to chance

TABLE 1

Intercorrelations, validity coefficients, and beta weights for four predictor variables from pre-flight against a pass-fail criterion from flight training [*]

	LDR	ACE	OLQ	FAV	Pass-fail crit. ($r_{bis.}$)	B wt.
Peer nominations on leadership	—	(268) .30 **	(268) .55 **	(188) .50 **	.27 **	.207
ACE test (college level)		—	.17 **	(239) .43 **	.07	−.089
Officer-like-qualities grade			—	(239) .58 **	.18	−.066
Final average at pre-flight				—	.28 **	.252

** 1% Level   R = .33

[*] In each case, the correlation coefficients reported are positive. The numbers in parentheses indicate the number of cases upon which the r is based. All validity coefficients have an N of 211.

fluctuations. Superiors' ratings on qualities related to leadership (OLQ) yield a validity coefficient which is positive but non-significant statistically; its beta weight is of a relatively low order as well. Scores on the ACE Test appear to have quite limited predictive value against the criterion. On the whole, then, the validity coefficients and beta weights for final pre-flight average and peer nominations on leadership suggest that these two variables are of greatest relative validity among those considered from the pre-flight level of training. The multiple R obtained for these variables was calculated to be .33.

Discussion

Considering the highly select nature of the population from which the sample was drawn, the complexity of the criterion applied, and the time differential between the predictor and criterion variables, the multiple of .33 takes on stature. The fact, too, that under these conditions peer nominations on leadership should predict the criterion is still more surprising. While a coefficient of .27, accounting for approximately 7% of the variance, is not striking by itself, in relative terms it suggests that peer nominations at an early level of training may account for unique variance in predicting the criterion. A number of hypotheses are entertained below in an attempt to derive meaning from the obtained relationship.

In the first place, it may be asserted as a reasonable assumption that peer nominations on leadership reflect a cadet's social acceptance within the cadet group. Hence, those cadets who are low on leadership are apt to be social isolates as well. Their assimilation within cadet groups may be limited and their probability of successful completion of the total program may be diminished correspondingly. If it is further assumed, however, that such individuals are as likely to withdraw from training as they are to fail, it should follow that a validity coefficient for peer nominations taken against a *pass-withdraw* criterion should yield an approximation to the coefficient secured with the pass-fail criterion. A test of this hypothesis, by actual computation of this coefficient, yielded an r of .07; the hypothesis was accordingly rejected.

This leads to the consideration that perhaps a record of inadequate achievement at pre-flight, by the then *potential* failures, is of significance in determining their leadership scores. The correlation of .50 between final pre-flight average and peer nomination lends credence to the ascription of influence by the former variable on the latter. While this hypothesis is basically sound, it does not completely or satisfactorily speak to the question posed because of the weight which peer nominations achieve independently of final average.

Another point of departure, from a somewhat different frame of reference, is that the kind of person who assimilates well in cadet groups—and who may consequently be expected to secure leadership status—may be the same kind of person whom instructors in flight training react to favorably. This influence may be particularly felt when a cadet is in difficulty and is presented before a board of officers to determine whether he is to be failed from flight training. Should he impress the board favorably by certain subtle interpersonal mechanisms, he may unintentionally be accorded a more sympathetic hearing than others. Whether before a board such as this or on the flight line, it seems probable that there is some weight introduced in favor of the more verbally fluent and socially facile individual. It is quite conceivable, therefore, that the obtained predictive quality of peer nominations might be accounted for in terms of some pervasive value through training of social characteristics such as these.

From this discussion, the points made will be seen to fall within two categories of conjecture: first, that the complex "leadership qualities," as defined by peer nominations, subsumes individual characteristics which are intrinsically related to the successful completion of flight training; second, that peer nominations tap a facet of the individual which is also perceived and reacted to by those who *evaluate* his performance in flight training. These categories certainly need not be conceived of as mutually exclusive of one another.

Whatever factors may be found to underlie the relationship between peer nominations on leadership and the pass-fail criterion from flight training, it is fundamentally true that neither variable is of a simple, unidimensional structure. In order, therefore, to distill out their commonality in meaningful psychological terms, further research is indicated. It would appear reasonable to consider that the first step in such a direction should be to have nominators verbalize the criteria by which they make their judgments of leadership. Beyond this, it would also be desirable to undertake full-scale research with a peer-nomination form specific to the nominator's estimate of the nominee's potential for successful completion of flight training.

In any event, it seems likely that the peer-nomination technique may have utility far exceeding current practice or expectation. The "informed judgment" of group opinion might well be profitably exploited further.

Summary

A study was conducted to determine the relationship between peer nominations on leadership during pre-flight and a pass-fail criterion from Naval Air Training. At the end of three months of pre-flight training, nine sections of Naval Aviation Cadets, a sample of 268 cases, were asked to nominate members of their section as best or least qualified for a military leadership position. Leadership scores were derived for each cadet. Three other scores were also obtained for the cadets from the pre-flight level of training: ACE Test; Officer-Like-Qualities grade (OLQ), assigned by officers in charge; and final over-all pre-flight average (FAV). Biserial r's were computed for each of these variables against pass-fail criterion data from flight training. Appropriate beta weights were also derived and a multiple R calculated.

The findings of this study were these:

1. Peer nominations on leadership (LDR) predicted the pass-fail flight criterion at a significant level ($r = .27$).

2. However, final pre-flight average ($r = .28$) was of virtually equal value as a predictor.

3. Neither OLQ ($r = .18$) or ACE Test ($r = .07$) predicted the flight criterion significantly.

4. The multiple R for these four predictor variables against the criterion was .33. The beta weights obtained indicated that LDR and FAV were bearing the load of prediction.

It was concluded that peer nominations on leadership, at the pre-flight level, might hold unique variance in predicting the pass-fail flight criterion. This was tentatively held to be attributable to two considerations: first, peer nominations might subsume characteristics intrinsically related to success in flight training; and, second, that peer nominations might tap a facet of the individual which is also perceived and reacted to by those who evaluate performance in flight training. Some implications for subsequent research were delineated with the suggestion that this technique be applied further.

10

The reliability of peer nominations under various conditions of administration

Recent years have seen an increasing applied utilization of some form of peer-evaluation technique. In basic terms, this involves each group member's assessment of his peers on some identifiable quality or complex of characteristics which is either directly observable, or indirectly inferable, from personal interactions. Such individual assessments are then integrated into a composite score reflecting each person's standing within his group. The advantage of this technique appears to reside in its ability to tap data drawn from interpersonal contacts. Furthermore, it evidently yields results

Peer-evaluation measures have been subjected to numerous validity studies summarized in Chapter 8, which have established their predictive utility against various performance criteria. Although these do lend support to broader application, it is nevertheless true that several questions remain to be answered regarding optimum employment. Notable among these is the matter of factors affecting reliability.

Reprinted from the *Journal of Applied Psychology*, 1957, 41, 85-90, with permission of the publisher, the American Psychological Association.

Problem

The particular instrument of attention in this study was the peer nomination, one of the more widely used of the peer-evaluation techniques. Three core variables relating to the reliability of peer-nomination scores were specified for consideration: first, the length of time a group must have spent together before scores will approximate maximized reliability; second, the presence of any differential effects on reliability accruing from the use of forms with a "research" set as against those with a "real" set; and, finally, the variations in reliability which may be attributable to the nature of the quality on which the nominator is instructed to make nominations.

Method

SUBJECTS AND SETTING

The sample consisted of 23 sections of officer candidates entering the Naval Officer Candidate School in Newport, Rhode Island, during July 1955. The total N available exceeded 700 at the beginning of this study. The sections numbered approximately 30 each; there is no reason to suppose that assignment to these sections was on anything other than a random basis.

The program at the OCS is of sixteen weeks' duration, with an orientation week introduced before the actual onset of the training cycle. During this one-week period, student personnel are assigned to sections, receive books and clothing, take classification tests, receive orientation lectures, but do not attend formal classes, as such.

Except for a small minority drawn from the fleet—in this class numbering fewer than 5%—all of the students were graduates of four-year college programs. The mean age of this class was 22 years with only a minimal dispersion about this figure. Students at the OCS are selected according to rigorous mental and physical standards. All are volunteers and must agree to remain on active duty as officers for three years following the successful conclusion of training.

The previous work of Suci, Vallance, and Glickman (1954) established several points which bore upon the selection of instruments for this study. Their research indicates that ". . . ratings by peers based on either the behavior at OCS or projected, future behavior are equally reliable . . ." (p. 11); in addition, they report that "The technique which requires selection of the upper and lower segments appears to have as satisfactory reliability as any of the other tested techniques . . ." (p. 11); finally, they note that the order of presentation which yields the lowest correlation between forms is "future officer" followed by "OCS behavior" (p. 12).

Four sociometric forms of the peer-nomination variety were utilized. Based upon the research just cited, a primary form calling for nominations on "success as a future Naval Officer" (FO) was administered to *all* sections. This form was seen to be of particular worth in its likely prediction of more distant, fleet performance criteria. In addition to this form, each section received *one of three* other forms, i.e. "leadership qualities" (LQ), "interest in and enthusiasm for the Naval Service" (IE),[1] and "probability of success in OCS" (OC). The selection of these forms rested upon a need to tap those characteristics which might relate to both in-training and post-training performance—i.e. interpersonal qualities, motivation, and ability having evident relevance to OCS performance.

Cutting across this pattern, approximately half the sections received a "research" set with the explicit point, appearing on their peer-nomination forms, that "The results of these ratings are to be used for research purposes only and will *not* affect your Navy career" (the so-called "RO" set). The other sections were given equally explicit instructions that "The results of these ratings may

---

[1] This particular form was derived from a study by Webb and Hollander, on the prediction of voluntary withdrawal from flight training as a morale criterion reported more fully in Chapter 13.

be used for administrative purposes" (the "AU" set). This split in treatment was designed to provide data on any differential effects attributable to administration under a "research" set, as against an "administrative" set, for all *four* forms.

In all there were *eight* possible treatments, i.e. four characteristics to be rated times two sets. All of the forms administered required *five* "high" and *five* "low" nominations in order of preference. An alphabetical section roster was attached.

DESIGN

The 23 sections were divided into six blocks of four sections each, except for one block which, of necessity, was limited to three sections. Sections were assigned to blocks on a rotation basis from the five companies in the second battalion. Such differences as might exist between companies were thus restricted in their conceivable ability to contaminate the study design.

Once having been assigned to a given block, the treatment of any given section was identical through training. Three major administrations of these forms were carried on during the training cycle: the first occurred during the so-called "orientation week" after the subjects had been together in their respective sections for four to five days; the second at the end of the third week of training; and the third at the end of the sixth week of training. The design was replicated, therefore, a total of three times. At the end of the thirteenth week of training, another administration was made, but this last time only the FO form was used. In all other respects, the design was identical for the latter administration.

SCORING

Following the pattern utilized in several studies elsewhere (cf. Hollander, 1954a), a direct weighting procedure was applied to derive peer-nomination scores. The highest nominee was awarded $+5$, the next highest a $+4$, and so on through the five "highs"; similarly, the lowest nominee was assigned a -5, the next lowest -4, and so on. An algebraic sum was then obtained for each subject and divided by the N of the group -1, since no subject may nominate himself. This results in an average score ranging on a continuum from $+5$ to -5. To remove the minus sign, a constant of 5 was added to this score; the resultant value was then multiplied by 10 in order to permit the use of a two-digit score without the intervening decimal point. Where a subject had an average raw value of -5, and hence a score of 00, he was arbitrarily given a score of 01, after the constant had been added and the multiplication had taken place. At the other end of the range, the $+5$ subject was given a score of 99, rather than 100.

The distribution arising from this procedure has normal characteristics with a range from 1 to 99, a mean of 50, and a standard deviation approximating 10, for the total population of the study. While this score may be seen to have certain features of a standard score, it does not tend to obscure section differences so much as does the standard score.

Results and discussion

Two major approaches may be followed in determining the reliability of peer-nomination data. In the first place, one may focus attention on the internal consistency of the nominations made within a given group at some discrete point in time. In the second place, one may deal with their consistency over time, as reflected in repeat administration (cf. Anderhalter, et al., 1952, p. 14).

Of the two approaches, the former is more usually applied. The latter one has evident disadvantages in that time exposure is very likely to have an impact in altering the position of subjects on the status continuum. This raises the question of whether, indeed, a "good" peer-nomination form ought to have high repeat reliability; in point of fact, one might wish to use peer nominations precisely for a study of temporal fluctuations in status, as well as the extent to which status is maintained. Thus, a low-level correlation between scores yielded by two administrations of the same peer-nomination form is very often evidence of an unstable group pattern, or unstable individual behavior, rather than of an inherent unreliability attributable to the form itself.

For our own purposes, we find both varieties of reliability of concern since we shall wish to know the internal consistency of scores obtained from various forms at various times, and the relationship over time of scores obtained from two administrations of the same form. Accordingly, both approaches were used in this study.

In practice, the calculation of single-stage reliability, or internal consistency, of a peer-nomination score is normally undertaken by an odd-even split of the raters within the group so as to afford two measures of status. The correlation between these measures is then treated by the Spearman-Brown formula to yield a corrected reliability coefficient.

Table 1 reports the corrected split-half reliability coefficients calculated at various points in the life cycle of relevant groups for the eight peer-nomination scores. The reduced N's reported were based upon a random selection of representative sections receiving the treatments involved. The identical sections are studied at each time period so as to control section variations which might obscure time effects. There is good reason to believe from cross analyses that these sections are literally representative of their treatment block.

It will be seen that the reliabilities in the first column, for all treatments, approximate .90—even though the sections had been comprised only four or five days before. Omitting considerations of validity, it is striking to note the rapidity with which a group perception of individuals appears to have crystallized. This high reliability is of particular note when one considers that previous studies, based upon peer-nomination scores drawn from later weeks of training, show r's which are not significantly greater. This is also reflected in our data here.

The yield, as regards higher reliabilities, is greater, but not significantly so, as one proceeds to later time periods. It would appear that the major increase occurs from the orientation week to the third week, after which the coefficients are stabilized. This is particularly discernible in the case of the FO forms which were carried through to a thirteenth-week administration.

With respect to the reliability of comparable forms administered under a "research" (RO) as opposed to an "administrative" (AU) set, no differences of a significant magnitude may be noted at any time level. Their respective patterns are practically identical.

TABLE 1

Corrected split-half reliabilities of eight peer-nomination treatments at various stages of training

Treatment by forms and sets	Week in training			
	Orientation week	Third week	Sixth week	Thirteenth week
"Future Officer"	.94	.97	.97	.97
Research set	96 *	92	91	91
"Future Officer"	.94	.97	.97	.95
Administrative set	96	96	95	91
"Interest and enthusiasm"	.91	.96	.96	
Research set	32	29	29	
"Interest and enthusiasm"	.88	.89	.94	
Administrative set	32	32	32	
"Success in OCS"	.93	.98	.99	
Research set	32	31	31	
"Success in OCS"	.89	.97	.98	
Administrative set	32	32	31	
"Leadership qualities"	.93	.96	.96	
Research set	32	32	31	
"Leadership qualities"	.94	.97	.98	
Administrative set	32	32	32	

* The number below each coefficient indicates the N upon which it is based

A contrast between the intercorrelation of scores for the "future officer" form, administered at various stages, under a research set as against an administrative set is to be seen in Table 2. In most respects the matrices are quite similar. Both indicate a sequential decrease in correlation between the orientation-week scores and those scores obtained from later administrations; both are notable for the high correlation, i.e. .90 and .94 respectively, between scores derived from the third- and sixth-week administrations; and, in general, both reflect a stability of measure from the third-week administration onward.

TABLE 2

Intercorrelation of peer-nomination scores for the "Future Officer" form administered under two sets independently at four stages of training

	"Future Officer"—research set		
	"3" week	"6" week	"13" week
"0" week	.74	.61	.53
		.78 *	
"3" week	—	.90	.81
"6" week		—	.88
	N throughout = 349		
	"Future Officer"—administrative set		
	"3" week	"6" week	"13" week
"0" week	.72	.65	.56
		.81 *	
"3" week	—	.94	.83
"6" week		—	.91
	N throughout = 320		

These average r's were calculated from the triad by application of Fisher's z transformation.

Tables 3, 4, and 5 follow on the pattern established in Table 2. In each case two matrices are provided—one for the research set and one for the administrative set—indicating the intercorrelation of *comparable forms* administered at three time levels. Paired comparison of comparable coefficients in the upper and lower matrices of each of these four tables yields *t* values which are not statistically significant. A high relationship (about .90) is revealed between third- and sixth-week nomination scores for all forms. An average intercorrelation for each triad, using a *z* transformation of *r*'s was computed. These average *r*'s are presented in the center of each triad. A *t* test of these reveals no significant difference *between sets* for any of the forms, including FO, where only its first three administrations were considered.

TABLE 3

Intercorrelation of peer-nomination scores for the "Interest and enthusiasm" form administered under two sets independently at three stages of training

"Interest and enthusiasm"—research set		
	"3" week	"6" week
"0" week	.78	.70
	.82 *	
"3" week		.91
N throughout = 119		

"Interest and enthusiasm"—administrative set		
	"3" week	"6" week
"0" week	.71	.63
	.76 *	
"3" week		.87
N throughout = 116		

* These average *r*'s were calculated from the triad by application of Fisher's transformation.

TABLE 4

Intercorrelation of peer-nomination scores for the "Success in OCS" form administered under two sets independently at three stages of training

	"Success in OCS"—research set	
	"3" week	"6" week
"0" week	.59	.40
	.68 *	
"3" week		.88
	N throughout = 112	

	"Success in OCS"—administrative set	
	"3" week	"6" week
"0" week	.65	.50
	.74 *	
"3" week		.91
	N throughout = 82	

These average r's were calculated from the triad by application of Fisher's z transformation.

Of all the forms, LQ evidences the highest average intercorrelation of the three scores. This is significantly greater for LQ-RO against OC-RO, and for LQ-AU against both OC-AU and IE-AU ($p < .05$). If any one form is to be considered to yield the most consistent score over time, then this is the LQ form. Since the evidence is somewhat spotty, and since consistency may have its limitations, it would not do to suggest that the LQ is perforce the "best" form.

It should also be noted, in this regard, that the LQ scores have substantially higher intercorrelation with FO scores at each time period than do either IE scores or OC scores ($p < .01$). From the magnitude of the r's involved (about .90), it would appear that the FO and LQ forms are being perceived as essentially similar.

Regrettably, the design of the study did not permit a complete matrix of intercorrelations among forms, although we have attained some picture of this from validity data reported in Chapter 11.

TABLE 5

Intercorrelation of peer-nomination scores for the "Leadership qualities" form administered under two sets independently at three stages of training

	"Leadership qualities"—research set	
	"3" week	"6" week
"o" week	.82	.77
	.87 *	
"3" week		.94
	N throughout = 118	

	"Leadership qualities"—administrative set	
	"3" week	"6" week
"o" week	.85	.78
	.88 *	
"3" week		.95
	N throughout = 122	

* These average r's were calculated from the triad by application of Fisher's transformation.

Conclusions

The data available from both varieties of reliability determination are essentially mutually supportive. The internal consistency measure is high throughout the time sequence. Early nominations manifest a significant relationship to later nominations, by the same groups, with the same forms. By the third week—and perhaps sooner, had we taken a sounding then—the nomination score stabilized, at least insofar as its correlation with the sixth-week score is concerned.

Of particular interest is the question of the eventual worth of the very early, i.e. orientation week, ratings obtained here. While their relationship to later ratings is high, there is certainly not a one-to-one correspondence evident. That this should be so is understandable in view of the greater range of information available to the rater at later stages. Indeed, we may speculate that the essential virtue of the early rating is that it is based upon personal contact *without* the direct intrusion of academic performance considerations, which usually correlate appreciably with peer nominations in settings of this kind.

In this regard it is of interest to note the high temporal stability of the leadership rating, which tends to be founded in an "interpersonal quality" rather than an academically loaded performance characteristic. Again, what this means in validity terms is an open question for the time. It is probable, however, that this has implications regarding the contribution of unique variance in the prediction of more ultimate criteria. Added to this picture, too, is the relatively lower average intercorrelation of the "success in OCS" scores, which are very likely subject to a greater degree of immediately observable fluctuations in classroom performance.

Since the "future officer" score reveals an average intercorrelation with itself which is roughly intermediate for the range set by the other forms (LQ, OC, and IE), we may infer that it is sensitive to a broader range of impressions than the "leadership qualities" score, at one extreme, or the "success in OCS" score, at the other. This seems understandable in view of the extrapolation required to a distant, and possibly diffuse, criterion.

The differences obtained between the administrative and research sets are minimal as regards any gain in reliability using one opposed to the other. Among other points, it may be suggested that results already obtained from peer-nomination studies, where research set was involved, may be taken to have "real life" implications. A caution must be introduced, however, lest premature conclusions are drawn regarding the differential validity of forms administered under these two sets.

Summary

From research conducted with 23 trainee sections at the Naval OCS in Newport, data are presented relative to the reliability of peer-nomination scores as it is affected by three variables: the period of time the group has spent together; the nature of the set given, i.e. "for research purposes" or "for administrative purposes"; and the quality or characteristic to be evaluated by the nominator in making his nominations.

It was found that the corrected split-half reliability of scores from forms administered very early in training, after the groups had been together for four to five days, was a reasonable approximation of the reliability obtained with the same forms and the same groups at later points in training. All forms showed a tendency to begin with subsequent reliability and to rise in subsequent administrations to only a slightly higher plateau.

The peer-nomination scores obtained at the end of the third week of training correlated at about the .90 level with those score obtained on the same groups at a later time, i.e. the sixth week.

There was no significant difference in the single-stage reliability or longitudinal reliability of comparable forms administered under the "research" as against the "administrative" set.

It was concluded that a peer nomination administered at the third week of training—or even earlier—will yield substantially the same information as that which is now obtained at considerably later points in time. Furthermore, it was noted that the "administrative" set leads to neither more nor less reliable scores than those secured through the presumably less threatening, or more lightly taken, "research" set.

11

The validity of early peer nominations

One of the most persistent concerns regarding the peer-nomination technique is the earliest point at which individuals have had a sufficient degree of exposure to one another so that their ratings will be of a reliable and valid nature.

In characteristically intensive training programs, like the military Officer Candidate School (OCS), this issue is of more than passing concern since peer nominations are expected to provide supplemental data for use in the evaluation and screening of trainees. The earlier such data are available, the more utility they may have as contributors to this process; this view is bolstered by the compelling consideration that prompt identification of marginal trainees can realize an appreciable saving in human terms of effort and disappointment as well as in terms of time and expense.

Problem

As part of a larger study of peer nominations reported in the preceding chapter, the aspect to be reported here was designed to shed light specifically on the comparative reliability and validity of peer-

Adapted in part from *Psychological Reports*, 1956, 2, 445-448, with permission the publisher.

nomination scores derived from forms administered early in the OCS training program.

Method

The data for the first stage of this study were gathered in 1955 at the Naval Officer Candidate School in Newport, Rhode Island, utilizing 23 trainee sections comprising an entire OCS class. Individuals had been assigned to these sections on a random basis and the total N available exceeded 700 at the outset of the project. Sections characteristically were about 30 in number.

As previously reported, there were four basic peer-nomination forms utilized. Each one required 5 "high" and 5 "low" peer nominations. One form, requiring nomination for "success as a future Naval Officer" (FO) was administered to *all* sections. This was presumed to have likely desirability in predicting a more distant fleet performance criterion. About this we shall have more to say in due course.

Each of the other three forms was administered to roughly a third of the sections comprising the sample. These were: "leadership qualities" (LQ); and "interest in and enthusiasm for the Naval Service" (IE); and "probability of success in OCS" (OCS). Thus, two forms—the FO plus one of the other three—were administered to any given section. Administrations were carried out three times during the training cycle, i.e. at the orientation, third, and sixth weeks. Sections consistently received the same forms at all three administrations.

Peer-nomination scores were derived through a rating procedure described in the preceding chapter. This involves the algebraic summation of plus and minus weights yielding a distribution normal character.

From among the candidates in the original study, 629 were identified who had gone on to duty as officers for periods averaging three years or more. For these people, fitness report ratings given by their senior officers were obtained and averaged to yield a score reflecting a composite of their fleet performance. Such ratings are given no less than once every six months as a routine procedure. The part of the rating form used was that requiring comparison with other officers of the same rank as the ratee.

Findings

As indicated in the chapter above, the split-half reliabilities for orientation week nomination scores, secured after no more than 4 or 5 days of contact, yielded values which were reasonable approximations to those of the later scores. For all forms, these early ratings achieve corrected values at or near .90. While some rise in the magnitude of these values was evident through the next two administrations, that increase was not statistically significant.

For validity, it was necessary in the first place to use the criterion most accessible at the OCS level. For all forms, at every stage, significant prediction of two in-training criteria was obtained. Thus, each of these peer-nomination scores gave correlations of a significant value with the military aptitude grades assigned by the officer personnel in charge of trainee companies. In terms of the comparative validity of forms, however, the LQ form was found to be a significantly better predictor ($P < .05$) of this criterion than OC, for the third and sixth week scores; other comparisons of forms did not manifest significant differences.

In predicting the final academic average criterion from OCS, the OC form was significantly superior to the other forms. It should be noted that this form yielded significant prediction of the academic criterion ($P < .01$) from the orientation week on. That this form should correlate significantly with academic performance, when it is administered at later stages of training, is not at all surprising in view of the persisting availability to raters of classroom performance data, coupled with the understandable impression that the factor represented is related to "success in OCS." It *is* striking, however, that during those first days of contact, before any academic work was undertaken, impressions were gained which led to significant prediction of the eventual, over-all academic performance of the individual. Finally, it should be noted that all forms tended to increase in correlation with academic performance over time. The prediction of this in-training criterion at the sixth week level did not differ significantly from predictions at the third week level so that no gain in validity was achieved as a consequence of delaying administration to the sixth week.

For the prediction of the fleet performance criterion, the "future officer" form from the third week of training yielded an average validity coefficient of .40. This value was not exceeded for the sixth week administration, thus demonstrating the success of this early evaluation in predicting later performance as an officer. How noteworthy this is may be seen from the consideration that the final military aptitude grade assigned by superiors in training correlated only .11 with this same criterion. Even the peer-nomination score from nominations on the "future officer" form during the orientation week did significantly better, with a validity coefficient of .24. Indeed, the only predictor from OCS achieving a degree of validity near the third week nomination score was the final academic average with a coefficient of .41 against the fleet criterion.

The third week peer-nomination score and the academic average are correlated .42 so that a partial r for peer nomination with fleet performance, holding the academic average constant, yields a value of .28; making use of a multiple r for the third week peer-nomination score, academic average, and an ability test of mathematics given at the beginning of training, a value of .51 is secured in predicting this distant criterion generated over several years. Thus early nominations hold up well in providing additional information concerning later performance, as previously found in the West Point follow-up studies noted in Chapter 8.

Discussion

In terms of reliability and validity, early peer nominations yield a stable and adequate approximation to the prediction obtainable from later nominations. This holds true even for the very earliest ratings, at the orientation week, in predicting post-training criterion data. There is reason to contend therefore that the central virtue of these early evaluations, taking account of their reliability, is that they are based upon personal contact *without* the direct intrusion of academic performance considerations. Perhaps they have value in contributing unique variance precisely because they are largely unaffected by the greater range of potentially contaminating information available to the rater at later points in training.

On this same point, it is of interest to note the high stability of "future officer" and "leadership qualities" nominations, which tend to be founded in an interpersonal quality rather than an academically-loaded performance characteristic. In contrast to this we see the relatively low average intercorrelation of the OC scores, a condition probably attributable to discernible fluctuations in classroom performance.

Summary and conclusions

A study of the reliability and differential validity of various peer nominations made in an OCS setting indicated that early nominations adequately approximated later ones. As a practical matter, there appears to be evidence here to support the discriminating use of early peer nominations in similar settings in order to gather supplemental data for the prediction of more distant criteria.

12

The friendship factor in peer nominations

One source of skepticism regarding the use of peer nominations as a quantification technique is the contention that friendship acts to bias the ratings assigned. Thus, in the case of "high" nominations, it is asserted that those named are more likely than not to be friends. If indeed nominations are biased by friendship ties, the metric derived would be an index of popularity more than an evaluation of some performance characteristic. Accordingly, ultimate prediction, in the usual validity sense, is menaced by this presumably contaminating influence.

Implicit in this indictment are several assumptions particularly worthy of note: first, that nominators will be more inclined to favor friends as "high" nominees; second, that this bias toward friends will operate independently of the characteristic to be considered, so long as it is a virtuous one; third, that the peer-nomination score consequently will be weighted with popularity; and fourth, that this is a bad state of affairs.

Certain of these points have already been dealt with in previous research. The work of Wherry and Fryer (1949), for example, has served to illuminate the predictive ability of a peer evaluation

Adapted from *Personnel Psychology*, 1956, 9, 435-447, with permission of the publisher.

technique as measured by external criteria. And, in point of fact, a variety of other studies have yielded substantially similar findings. More directly, perhaps, the study by Hollander and Webb, presented in Chapter 6, has demonstrated that there is nowhere near a one-to-one relationship between choice as a friend and nomination as "high" on a peer evaluation. Furthermore, this same study indicates that differing numbers of friends are nominated "high," on the average, depending upon the characteristic set for evaluation. It should be noted, too, that an aggregate "friendship score," taken as an index of popularity, shows a varying relationship to the two characteristics studied, i.e. leadership and followership.

Problem

The essence of the matter would seem to be whether the so-called friendship factor does indeed limit the validity of peer-nomination scores. In the current study, we shall consider the relationship of individual friendship choice to "high" nominations, and the relationship of aggregate friendship choice to peer-nomination scores and a criterion of performance.

In particular, we shall view these relationships as they may vary depending upon the form involved, the reality element in the instructional set, and the time of administration, in the sense of the group's life-span since formation.

Method

SUBJECTS AND SETTING

The sample consisted of 23 sections of officer candidates entering the Newport Naval Officer Candidate School during July 1955. The total N available for study exceeded 700, at the beginning of this study. Sections numbered approximately 30 each; and assignment to these was on a random basis. Other conditions of selection and training are reported in the two foregoing chapters.

INSTRUMENTS

Four key sociometric forms of the peer-nomination variety were utilized. Based upon previous research conducted at Newport (Suci, *et al.*, 1954), a primary form calling for nominations on "success as a future Naval Officer" (FO) was administered to *all* sections. This form was seen to be of particular worth in its likely prediction of more distant, fleet performance criteria. In addition to this primary form, each section received *one of three* so-called secondary forms, i.e. "leadership qualities" (LQ), "interest in and enthusiasm for the Naval Service" (IE), and "probability of success in OCS" (OC). The selection of these forms rested upon a need to tap those characteristics which might relate to both in-training and post-training performance—i.e. interpersonal qualities, motivation, and ability having evident relevance to OCS performance.

Cutting across this pattern, approximately half the sections received a "research" set with the explicit point, appearing on their peer-nomination forms, that "The results of these ratings are to be used for research purposes only and will *not* affect your Navy career." The other sections were given equally explicit instructions that "The results of these ratings may be used for administrative purposes." This split in treatment was designed to provide data on any differential effects attributable to administration under a "research" set (RO) as against an "administrative" set (AU).

As described in the preceding chapters, there were eight possible treatments, i.e. four characteristics to be rated times two sets. All of the forms required five "high" and five "low" nominations in order of preference. An alphabetical section roster was attached.

In addition to this basic pattern, at the close of every administration, each subject was asked to list five people in his section who were actual or potential friends; a "research" set was used exclusively in the administration of this form.

DESIGN

The 23 sections were divided into six blocks of four sections each, except for one block which, of necessity, was limited to three sections. Sections were assigned to blocks on a rotation basis from the five companies in the second battalion. Such differences as might exist between companies were thus restricted in their possible ability to contaminate the study design.

Once having been assigned to a given block, the treatment of any given section was identical through training. Three major administrations of these forms were carried on during the training cycle: the first occurred during the so-called "orientation week" after the subjects had been together in their respective sections for four to five days; at the end of the third week of training; and at the end of the sixth week of training. The design was replicated, therefore, a total of three times. At the end of the 13th week of training, another administration of forms was made, but this last time only the primary, "future officer" form was used. In all other respects, the design was identical for the latter administration.

SCORING

A direct weighting procedure was applied to derive peer-nomination scores. The highest nominee was awarded a +5, the next highest, a +4, and so on through the five "highs"; similarly, the lowest nominee was assigned a −5, the next lowest, a −4, and so on. An algebraic sum was then obtained which was subsequently treated so as to yield a positive, two-digit score reflecting the status of the individual in his section.

Friendship scores were derived by a simple summation of people choosing the subject. This may be taken as a kind of "popularity index," although it is subject to instability, as might be anticipated.

RELIABILITY

As reported in Chapter 10, the corrected single-stage reliabilities of the peer-nomination scores approximate .90, even where the sections have been together only during the orientation week.

Thus, there is no significant gain in reliability at the later time levels. As regards repeat reliability, scores obtained from the same form administered at different time levels show a high sequential intercorrelation, particularly for third and sixth week readings.

Odd-even reliabilities for the friendship score, when corrected, vary from .50 at the orientation week to .66 at the thirteenth week, with an N of some 120 subjects representing four randomly-selected sections. Considering its highly idiosyncratic nature, the low reliabilities for friendship are not surprising.

Results and discussion

Paralleling the analysis in Chapter 6, Table 1 presents the mean number of friends chosen "high" on different peer-nomination forms, at three time levels, under two sets. Over-all, the data reveal that about two out of the five acknowledged friends named by each subject are nominated, on the average, as his "high" nominees. It would not do to suggest that this reveals no bias in favor of friends; clearly, with five "high" choices to be made, among roughly thirty people, there is significance in the fact that even an average of two out of five friends appear among these five. Yet this is by no means a total correspondence. Moreover, it remains to be determined whether those friends who are nominated "high" might not be deserving of this status.

To gain a picture of the relationships at play in Table 1, an analysis of variance was completed and is summarized in Table 2. The limiting feature of this analysis was the assumption of one case per cell, necessitated in part by the variant N's involved and the conceivable contamination introduced by FO's correlation with other forms. While it is true that this diminishes power, it has the virtue of demanding more marked differences to yield significance; thus, F ratios which are significant may be considered to be so under a handicap. The analysis, therefore, is highly conservative in the direction of rendering nonsignificant findings.

TABLE 1

Mean frequency of friends chosen high for eight peer-nomination treatments at various stages of training

Treatment by forms and sets	Week in training		
	Orientation week	Third week	Sixth week
FO-RO	2.46	2.19	2.24
	385 *	382	374
FO-AU	2.36	2.18	2.09
	354	357	348
IE-RO	1.98	1.58	1.50
	130	127	125
IE-AU	1.92	1.72	1.69
	129	131	128
OC-RO	1.85	1.60	1.63
	126	125	123
OC-AU	1.97	1.77	1.39
	95	96	92
LQ-RO	2.29	2.02	2.10
	129	130	126
LQ-AU	2.37	1.90	1.97
	130	130	128

* The figure beneath each mean indicates the number of nominators upon which the mean is based.

Study of Table 2 reveals that both form and time yield significant independent effects, while set does not. Pursuing these points, we find that significantly fewer friends (1% level) are nominated as "high" on IE and OC than are so nominated on FO and LQ. It would appear, then, that friends are more readily seen to have leadership qualities or future officer potential than they are seen to have interest and enthusiasm in the Naval Service or a high probability of success in OCS. One may view this, in part, as an index of the relative value assigned these characteristics in friendship choice itself—or, more basically, as a likely sign of the motivation pattern among officer candidates circa 1955.

TABLE 2

Summary of analysis of variance for Table 1 with assumption of one case per cell

Source	Sum of squares	df	Mean square	F
(1) Form	1.3585	3	.4528	39.50 * (from 7)
(2) Time	.4937	2	.2469	21.28 * (from 7)
(3) Set	.0005	1	.0005	—
(4) F x T	.0398	6	.0066	—
(5) T x S	.0174	2	.0087	—
(6) F x S	.0282	3	.0094	—
(7) Residual	.0696	6	.0116	
Total	2.0077	23		

* 1% level.

Over time, the data in Table 1 indicate that significantly more friends (1% level) are nominated as "high" on the various forms at the orientation week than are so nominated either at the third or the sixth week of training; the latter two readings are not significantly different from one another. It may be suggested that the higher means for the first reading are accountable in terms of relatively fewer contacts and a resultant dependence upon friends' names.

In Table 3 correlation coefficients between friendship scores and various peer-nomination scores are provided. It will be seen that all of these coefficients are significant beyond the 1% level, thus revealing that peer-nomination scores do reflect "popularity."

TABLE 3

Correlation between friendship scores and eight peer-nomination treatments at various stages of training

Treatment by forms and sets	Week in training			
	Orientation week	Third week	Sixth week	Thirteenth week
FO-RO	.56	.58	.64	.63
	388 *	382	374	358
FO-AU	.54	.58	.57	.66
	354	357	348	324
IE-RO	.45	.26	.37	
	130	127	125	
IE-AU	.45	.45	.54	
	129	131	128	
OC-RO	.36	.37	.38	
	128	125	123	
OC-AU	.48	.40	.34	
	95	96	92	
LQ-RO	.62	.64	.62	
	130	130	126	
LQ-AU	.64	.57	.58	
	130	130	128	

Note: All of the above coefficients are significant beyond the 1% level.
* The number beneath each coefficient indicates the N upon which it is based.

Using the first three columns in this table, an analysis of variance of coefficients was completed following their transformation to Fisher's z function. Once having been thus treated, these coefficients may be viewed as any other numbers. Table 4 summarizes this analysis. Since the N's upon which the coefficients were initially based have been obscured by this treatment, the outcome leans toward the conservative side. The consequences of this approach have been considered above.

Among the variables involved, only the independent effect of form is significant. Returning to Table 3, it is found that, in general, FO and LQ yield a significantly higher relationship (1% level) with the friendship score than do IE or OC. This duplicates the findings of the analysis completed with Table 1.

TABLE 4

Summary of analysis of variance for Table 3: following z transformation of correlation coefficients

Source	Sum of squares	df	Mean square	F
(1) Form	.4118	3	.1373	27.46 * (from 7)
(2) Time	.0062	2	.0031	—
(3) Set	.0026	1	.0026	—
(4) F x T	.0275	6	.0046	—
(5) T x S	.0020	2	.0010	—
(6) F x S	.0362	3	.0121	2.42 † (from 7)
(7) Residual	.0302	6	.0050	
Total	.5165	23		

* 1% level.
† Not significant.

In order to provide a foundation for ascertaining the effect of the friendship score on validity, this score was correlated, by treatment block, with final OCS academic average as a basic, in-training criterion. At the orientation week level, coefficients range about zero, with an average at that point; at the third week level, all coefficients have a positive sign and range from .01 to .27, with an average of .13; at the sixth week level, this average reaches .17; and, at the thirteenth week level is .19 (Hollander, 1956c, p. 16). There is no systematic pattern in evidence, other than this progressive increase in magnitude over time. Coefficients for the "research" set are not significantly different from those obtained under the "administrative" set.

The ultimate problem of limitation of validity is covered by the data of Table 5. With the availability of the coefficients discussed and the peer-nomination validity coefficients against the academic criterion, it was possible to partial the effect of friendship so as to obtain "purified" validities. In Table 5, original validities are given with their corrected value indicated in parentheses. While upward and downward changes are manifested, the global picture is one of stability. No coefficients are significantly altered by the partialing process; the differential level of prediction, for various treatments, and at various times, remains substantially the same.

TABLE 5

Validity coefficients against final OCS academic average for eight peer-nomination treatments at various stages of training with corrected values after partialing of friendship scores

Treatment by forms and sets	N	Week in training			
		Orientation week	Third week	Sixth week	Thirteenth week
FO-RO	349	.15† (.17)	.46† (.46)	.51† (.51)	.47† (.45)
FO-AU	320	.12* (.15)	.39† (.41)	.40† (.41)	.41† (.41)
IE-RO	119	.05 (.05)	.22* (.21)	.16 (.12)	
IE-AU	116	.29† (.36)	.41† (.40)	.30† (.27)	
OC-RO	112	.31† (.37)	.70† (.71)	.73† (.70)	
OC-AU	82	.32† (.34)	.74† (.73)	.83† (.83)	
LQ-RO	118	.29† (.26)	.45† (.37)	.54† (.49)	
LQ-AU	122	.10 (.07)	.22* (.31)	.25† (.25)	

* 5% level.
† 1% level.

Conclusions

In broad terms, the results obtained do not support the contention that friendship operates as an adversely biasing and invalidat-
ing factor in peer nominations. It is true, of course, that friends
do receive a somewhat larger number of "high" nominations than
their actual proportion would indicate. But the aggregative effect
of this—in the popularity sense—does not lead to a generalized
diminution of validity. Thus, though popularity tends to be functionally related to peer-nomination scores, this fails to alter prediction fundamentally.

One of the more intriguing outgrowths of these results is the
suggestion offered for a redirection of emphasis. Perhaps this apparent favoring of friends does not serve to create status so much as
it reflects a desire to have as friends those who are already manifestly high on valued status continua. The basis for this, in the
sense of an interrelationship of sociometric status continua, has
already been observed in the work of Lemann and Solomon (1952).
The point here is that friendship choice may be a part function of
status, rather than status ascription a resultant of friendship. Thus,
at the very least, some friends who are nominated as "high" may
be clearly deserving of this status. There are several evident signs
which underpin this interpretation.

In the first place, friendship bears varying relationships to the
scores derived from the four peer-nomination forms studied. That
such an element of discrimination is present tends to contrain-
dicate the operation of a persistent bias in favor of friends; it also
introduces the consideration of value attached to differing continua. Second, the evidence reveals no significant differences in the
relationship of friendship to peer nominations for the "research"
as against the "administrative" set. One might have hypothesized
a differential biasing effect, if friendship acted as a prime element
in nominations.

There is another aspect to this, however, requiring consideration.
The substantial correlation of the friendship score with peer-

nomination scores, and the latter's validity after partialing of the former, demands further explication. It might be argued that, if the thesis were sound, the friendship score ought to diminish the correlation between peer-nomination scores and the criterion. This is predicated on the view that the friendship score itself should have validity against the criterion. That it does not is pragmatically significant, but also apparently at odds with the thesis. To account for this, it is only necessary to bear in mind that each nominator *must* name five friends; at the outset, then, this sets a constraint which may be viewed as the likely source of the low reliability of the friendship score, and its low validity, as well. While it could be, then, that friendship choice is still idiosyncratic, *some* of those five "friends" may well be high status individuals who ultimately constitute a goodly share of the average two out of five who are nominated as "high." It is well to recall here that there is no necessity to support the existence of a total identity between friendship choices and "high" nominees in order for the thesis to hold.

Related to this issue is the additional point that validity was narrowed to the prediction of but one kind of criterion. It could be that somewhat different patterns might have evidenced themselves had another criterion been applied. In addition, it is conceivable that the nature of the groups involved, and their training milieu, may have made a unique contribution to the findings.

At the heart of the matter, we may conclude that additional substance has been given the position that peer nominations provide quantification of characteristics without restrictive contamination from friendship bonds. It appears true still that this technique yields a good deal more by way of prediction than would a popularity contest.

Summary

One objection to the peer nomination is the contention that it produces ratings loaded with a friendship factor. This study presents data on this issue in terms of peer nominations administered in OCS. The results indicate that while friends appear to be favored somewhat for high nominations, peer nominations on performance characteristics have validity for in-training criteria without adverse effects from friendship.

13

Comparison of three morale measures:
A survey, pooled group judgments,
and self evaluations

WITH WILSE B. WEBB

That there are many ways of defining morale, and very little agreement about the best definition, is probably all too obvious. In his pertinent work, Viteles (1953) has been led to comment that generalizations regarding morale have suffered by "the almost consistent failure of surveys (and also of experimental studies) to deal with the problem within an appropriate context of theory ... the most usual tendency has been to define the dimensions of morale in terms of what is revealed by the investigation" (p. 282).

As one turns attention to the actual measurement of morale, an understandably disjointed state of affairs presents itself. It may be suggested that three interrelated conditions underlie this situation: first, varying investigators have been prone to select a single dimension as a total definition of morale; second, few cross comparisons have been made of the measures reputedly tapping "morale";

Reprinted from the *Journal of Applied Psychology*, 1956, 40, 17-20, with permission of the publisher, the American Psychological Association.

third, too frequently the measurement taken has been accepted as valid without further reference to behavior.

Amid this turmoil, the attitude or questionnaire survey has continued to thrive as a singularly prominent technique of morale assessment. The healthy respect it has achieved has largely stemmed from its pragmatic utility in pinpointing causes of employee satisfaction or dissatisfaction. But this is not always enough, for the "morale index" resulting from such surveys has been noted, on occasion, to produce the apparent anomaly of a negative relationship between the presumably favorable responses and productivity records. A case in point is reported by Katz from the data yielded in a large-scale industrial study (1949, p. 160).

In contrast to the rather extensive use of various forms of the survey, only infrequent utilization has been made of self or coworker evaluation of individual morale. With the heightened popularity of such devices, and their relatively extended history in predicting behavioral criteria, the virtually exclusive reliance on the more traditional techniques is somewhat surprising.

Problem

Taking these considerations into account, it would appear desirable to initiate exploratory studies which would permit: (a) the determination of interrelationships between several, simultaneously produced indices of morale, oriented about a single, *common* definition; and (b) the evaluation of these measures as regards their relative validity against some suitable behavioral criterion of morale.

Procedure

Within the context of naval air training, morale was defined quite simply as "an interest in and enthusiasm for the naval air program." This definition was borrowed from one proposed by Smith and Westen (1951, p. 1) in their Air Force study. It implies a felt

need to succeed in, to be part of, and to contribute to naval aviation. Most significant, perhaps, it implies a desire to complete the
training curriculum, so far as personal desires operate to that end.
This definition was deemed particularly appropriate since (a)
measurement could be performed by the several methods suggested, and (b) it was practical in that measured differences might
logically result in variation in training proficiency.

On the basis of a long-standing interview study of trainee morale
(Bair & Hollander, 1953), a 20-item questionnaire was developed,
directed at probing attitudes which would reflect variations in
morale within the definition used. The items utilized were based
upon a thorough understanding of the problem areas in the training program. Prior to the development of this final form, a detailed
morale survey had been completed for the information of cogni-
zant authorities. The 20-item form ultimately used represented a
drawing out and refinement based on earlier analyses. There was
every reason to expect that this questionnaire suited the purposes
of this study by providing the most penetrating morale survey for
the population involved.

From previous work with the peer-nomination technique, reported in Chapter 8, a special form was developed on which each
cadet was asked to nominate, in order, the three men in his section
whom he considered "highest" on "interest in and enthusiasm for
naval aviation," and the three men whom he considered "lowest"
on this variable.

In addition to these measures, each cadet was asked to rank
himself on this interest and enthusiasm variable, in comparison
with his sectionmates, by inserting a number in a blank space.
Since this ranking was obtained on the same form as the peer nominations, it was presumed to be based upon substantially the same
psychological set.

All three of these devices were administered to eight cadet sections graduating from a four-month pre-flight curriculum at Pensacola in the winter of 1953-54. A total of 210 cases, with each section
composed of approximately 25 men, was thus obtained. The group

estimate of a cadet's morale was secured by weighting "high" nominations $+3$, $+2$, $+1$, and "low" nominations -3, -2, -1, and
then algebraically summing these weights. Fortunately, the problem of "unnominated" cases was minimal as only six cases fell in
this category. For each section, a rank-order score of cadets was
then developed. These data and the self-rank data were then converted to rankits to permit comparisons across sections.

The morale inventory was empirically scored by taking the 50
men having the highest peer-nomination score and the 50 men
having the lowest peer-nomination score and determining the
items of the morale survey which significantly discriminated between these groups on the basis of tetrachoric correlations. Twelve
items were found to yield such discrimination; the morale survey
was then scored for all subjects, using these 12 items. This procedure gave a score for the morale survey which was maximized in
the sense that it might have the highest possible correlation with
the other variables.

Estimates of the reliability of the morale survey and the peer
nominations were determined. An odd-even reliability for the survey form resulted in an average of .55 for the eight sections; when
corrected by the Spearman-Brown formula, this became a reliability
estimate of .71. An analysis of variance estimate of the reliability of
peer nominations yielded an r of .82.

Results

Table 1 provides the intercorrelations of the maximized morale
inventory score, the self ratings, and the peer nominations (or
group estimate) of morale. These intercorrelations were secured by
first determining the intrasection correlations and then averaging
these, taking into account the N of the groups involved. Although
the r's reported are significant, they are sufficiently low in magnitude to suggest that the measures used resulted in different estimates of a person's "morale," even when this concept of morale

was based upon a common definition. One may now ask which of these appears to best predict a performance criterion of morale.

In keeping with the definition set forth above, the simplest performance measure of morale which appeared appropriate was the pass-withdraw criterion, that is, whether the individual remained in training or *voluntarily* withdrew during a five-month period of flight training following pre-flight. During this period more than 90% of the voluntary withdrawal during flight training will occur.

TABLE 1

Intercorrelation of three estimates of morale

Variables	r
Self estimate vs. group estimate	.37 *
Survey estimate vs. group estimate	.40 *
Survey estimate vs. self estimate	.39 *

* $P < .01$

In Table 2 biserial correlations are presented for these three measures against this pass-withdraw criterion; 16 of the original 210 cases had withdrawn at this time. Because of the low proportion of cases in the withdrawal group, the standard errors of these biserials are, of course, considerable. In the light of this unavoidable but vexing problem, an additional correlational estimate was

TABLE 2

Validity coefficients against a pass-withdraw criterion for three estimates of morale

Predictor	r_{bis} with criterion	Kendall's Tau
Group estimate	.90	.27
Self estimate	.83	.22
Survey estimate	.30	.11

obtained using Kendall's Tau. These nonparametric estimates are also presented in Table 2. The actual extent of these correlations with the criterion of withdrawal will, of course, require further accumulation of cases from succeeding samples. However, our major concern with these coefficients was the relative relationships that they revealed.

As striking as the validities shown in Table 2 may be, a tabulation by quartiles of the withdrawal group, on the three measures applied, is perhaps even more impressive. A distribution of the 16 withdrawal cases falling in each quartile of the scores for each variable is given in Table 3. From a study of this table, it will be

TABLE 3

Quartile distributions on three estimates of morale for 16 withdrawal cases

	Self estimate	Group estimate	Survey estimate
Q_4 (upper 25%)	1	1	1
Q_3	1	1	5
Q_2	6	5	5
Q_1 (lower 25%)	8	9	5

noted that 50% of the men who subsequently withdrew were among the lower 25% of the estimates of the total sample. Nine of the 16 withdrawals had been judged by their peers as being in the lower 25% on the "interest and enthusiasm" variable. All of the estimates, when compared with the expected distribution of scores, show a tendency for withdrawals to have lower morale of the variety here defined than successful cadets.

It may be noted in passing that six cadets had been eliminated on grounds of "flight failure," i.e. being unable to learn to fly. Since these cases would primarily represent deficiencies in aptitude rather than motivation, we would expect little relationship between our measures and this condition. Such, in fact, was the case: on self ratings 50% placed the enthusiasm level as above the average of the group, 50% below the average; on group rating one-third of these cases were placed in the upper 50% of the ratings; the morale survey scores place two-thirds of these men above average in their favorable responses.

Discussion and conclusions

The findings presented may be interpreted to mean, first, that if we had tapped morale by one method rather than another, considerable variation in estimates of a given individual's "morale" within his group would have been obtained. This is so, even within the framework of the common definition applied. It lends reinforcement to the consideration that the most rigorous specification of the term is required. The implicit problem now posed might be which of these measures is a "true index" of the individual's morale.

In the introduction to this study it was suggested that the meaningfulness of a predictor of morale might be appropriately tested by its relationship to the reality of a performance criterion. It is evident from the second analysis that the measures obtained by peer nominations and self ratings *do* show a strong relationship to the pass-withdraw criterion derived from subsequent training. On the other hand, the survey estimate of morale bears only a relatively limited relationship to this criterion.

The findings that the group estimate yields a high estimate validity against this performance criterion, are not inordinately surprising in light of other evidence regarding the penetrating quality of pooled group judgments. It is totally reasonable to suppose that the members of a group, living together under intimate conditions for several months, might have a highly sophisticated "group understanding" of member characteristics. In a military setting such as this, where "interest and enthusiasm" are significant in day-to-day activity, this sophistication might be heightened all the more.

Considering the survey estimate, its relationship to the criterion is considerably lower than that evidenced by the other two measures. This finding may stem from two sources: the limitation of this specific survey form or a limitation which may be inherent in the survey instrument approach to morale, where the prediction of a performance criterion is involved. It may only be asserted in response to the first point that the survey employed was a refinement of one that had already demonstrated its operational utility of the traditional purposes. There was substantial reason to believe it totally adequate.

Without dispensing with the survey technique, therefore, it would seem that credence has been lent to the view that for purposes of predicting performance criteria of morale, self ratings and peer nominations may have considerable usefulness. It is, of course, true that such indices cannot be derived from simply *any* group but must be employed only under applicable conditions. While survey instruments may continue to provide cues to administrative action where morale is concerned, nevertheless, there is merit in considering the utilization of the peer-nomination or self-rating techniques for the handling of prediction problems of the sort encountered here.

Summary

A study was completed to determine the relative validity of three techniques of morale assessment in predicting an operational criterion in naval air training. Morale was defined simply as an "interest in and enthusiasm for naval aviation." An attitude survey, peer-nomination form, and self rating were used as the measuring instruments.

Eight sections of naval aviation cadets graduating from pre-flight ($N = 210$) were used as the study sample. Scores were derived for each of these measures and intercorrelated with one another. These coefficients were found to be of relatively low magnitude. As for their validities, it was found that group estimates ($r_{bis} = .90$) and self estimates ($r_{bis} = .83$) yielded the highest relative relationships with a criterion of pass-withdraw after five subsequent months of training. The coefficient for survey estimate was notably lower ($r_{bis} = .30$). Although the standard errors of these coefficients are largely due to an extreme split, their relative magnitude is informative.

The conclusion was offered that peer nominations and direct self descriptions may have greater utility in reflecting involvement in a training program than does the traditional "morale index" derived from a survey instrument.

IV

Leadership emergence, status, and conformity

Returning to the central conception of emergent leadership, this section presents further points about conformity and status as related influence processes. The first three chapters, Fourteen, Fifteen, and Sixteen, set forth the ideas essential to the "idiosyncrasy credit" concept and elaborate them in several directions.

Chapters Seventeen, Eighteen, and Nineteen report three successive experiments drawing upon that theoretical model. All reveal something of the interactive quality of person perception and the especially critical nature of process, sequence, and position in yielding responses to nonconforming behaviors. In each case refinements for the basic model are provided by this empirical work and these are extended to considerations in Chapter Twenty.

In that last chapter various materials in this book are brought to focus on the matter of effective leadership. While recognizing that there are no universal "traits of leadership," it is possible to speak of attributes and behaviors which generally have a place in effective leadership. Following some enumeration of these, implications are then drawn for the wider issue of influence as a general process.

14

Some points of reinterpretation regarding social conformity

Among those phenomena lying within the scope of social research, none occupies a more central place than conformity. Leaving aside the ugly connotations the term has garnered of late, a simple reality prevails: all individuals, in time, space, and degree, "conform"— if we mean by this that they alter the course of their behavior in keeping with social forces. This is plainly a basal requirement for social integration. A modifiability or plasticity of individual behavior is essential if society, any society, is to function smoothly.

That conformity is therefore of singular import may be granted readily, though limiting it as to definition and interpretation is still another matter. It is after all neither a persisting attribute of the individual nor just an isolated state through which he passes. Rather it is best considered as a complexly determined, episodic outcome of the ongoing social interaction between the individual and the "other people" with whom he is in contact at a time. And this interaction itself must be understood to comprise more than the literalist's view of people behaving reciprocally in time, for

Originally given as an invited address before the 1958 Annual Conference of the British Psychological Society at Birmingham, England, and reprinted here from *Sociological Review* (England), 1959, 7, 159-168, with permission of the publisher.

individuals are the carriers of what has transpired before, thus insuring that present interactions are being governed in part by the impressions remaining from past interactions.

The interplay of social and psychological elements accordingly contained in conformity calls forth the distinctive approach characterized by social psychology. This concerns itself with those attributes of the individual which relate to certain general classes of environmental variables producing social behavior. As illustrative points of departure, two problems especially demand attention regarding conformity: the individual psychological states which dispose toward manifest conformity; and, relatedly, the trustworthiness of manifest conformity as evidence of individual intent.

The last point serves as a particularly useful line to several central considerations here. For some time, conformity has been seen to depend upon some fixed norm to which all members of a group are expected to adhere; attractive and simple as it is, this notion misleads by deftly avoiding the verifiable truth that one man's act of "conformity" may be another's "nonconformity," depending upon how the others in that situation feel about each. By neglecting the perceiver and his impressions from the past, this static orientation encourages a fruitless quest for stable attributes of either the individual or the situation in generating conformity, based in a single snapshot of behavior at a set point in time.

Two levels of conformity behavior

Clarity may be introduced here by an initial distinction between conformity as a problem of process and one of effect. At the level of *process*, conformity should be accountable with regard to some motive impelling action. To say that an individual conforms just because others evidence a given behavior is to reach the *reductio ad absurdum* that he conforms because he conforms. Why must he care about the behavior of others? In the case of the child *vis-à-vis* the parent, we may speak with some reason about identification o "modeling behavior." But what of an adult placed among others in what we may call a group context? If we simply invoke imitation as a motive, then we are still obliged to explain a lack of generalized imitation (cf. Miller & Dollard, 1941; and Schein, 1954). Why the evident selectivity? People do not, in point of fact, conform to just any behavior displayed by others. Which leads us necessarily to inquire about the person's individual psychological states, particularly how his motives and percepts may direct conformity.

To illustrate the level of *effect*, recall that we readily observe in everyday contact that behavior accepted from one individual may not be nearly so acceptable from another. Or, turning it around, what we demand of one individual by way of conformity to some social standard we may not so strictly demand of another (see Homans, 1950, Ch. 16). This is often explained away by alluding to the rather loose designation "status." We acknowledge that some people have a certain something which alters our expectations, and tolerance, regarding their behavior. In what is to follow, more will be said about this operational aspect of status. For now, we may undertake a brief excursion into individual-to-group relationships, preparatory to a recasting of the problem.

Group contexts and interpersonal expectancies

As part of the movement away from the descriptive to a more analytic probing of group membership, there has emerged the concept of "reference group." This is a useful construct serving to account for the relevance of a group to an individual's behavior; it has to do with the consideration that both behavior and less apparent sorts of things, e.g. orientations in one's perception of the social environment, as in "attitudes," are tied to and elicited by the groups to which an individual refers himself; and that, most importantly, this even includes groups to which he does not belong, but to which he may aspire. Thus, noting membership is never sufficient in itself; we must know whether the individual actually "refers" himself to a group; this raises the question of whether he cares, or is motivated, to retain identification with the group at hand.

When we ask then why it is that one group guides an individual's behavior while another, to which he belongs, does not, or does less, we must seek ultimately an answer in rewards he finds from actual or implied interaction with them, disallowing, of course, cases of sheer physical coercion. Typically, the face-to-face group, affording interactions with concomitant communications, has particular importance as a source for the determination of group identifications. But, other communication sources, of a secondary nature, could fulfill this function.

In either event, by some direct or indirect mode of interaction, expectancies develop regarding behavior which are appropriate for the individual. Accordingly, as a neophyte in a group he would most probably take as a first approximation of these expectancies what others appear to be doing, and he might receive formal directives as well. Whether communicated explicitly or implicitly to him, however, these expectancies reside in perceptions of him held by others: thus, "we expect newcomers to know their place and hold their tongues."

When expectancies have normative character in the modal sense, i.e. where individual A is expected to behave in fashion X in situation Q by other individuals B, C, D, and so on, we may speak of "group expectancies." Behavior itself is not the normative element so much as the underlying expectancies of the group; further, we may consider that expectancies have reference to roles, highly specific behavior, as well as to norms, more general behavior (cf. Newcomb, 1950, and Bates, 1956).

An individual behaves appropriately within a given group framework by perceiving these expectancies. In the simplest case, he comes to find them ready guides to comfortable interaction, so much so that they become implicit to his behavior. One need not see this as a matter of deliberation; quite conceivably, a person may eventually incorporate a ready sense of the appropriate without conscious thought, if by this last term we mean verbal manipulation directed at problem solving.[1]

More to the point, an individual may strive very hard indeed—as in the classic case of the social-climber—to identify expectancies, those of the higher class, and fulfill these insofar as possible. The motivation of the individual to belong to the group therefore bears critically upon this process: the matter of recognizing expectancies must rest in some measure upon this motivation.

Two contributors to motivation to belong

The genesis of this inclusive "motive to belong" raises still other questions, not the least of which is the issue of its frequent conception as a unitary attribute of the individual. It would seem that, contrary arguments notwithstanding, much the sounder view is that a discrimination is properly demanded between attraction to a group (an adherence born of group function), and some individually-based motive for achieving social approval from the group members as a set of "relevant others."

These two distinctive motivational components may be subsumed within the general term; operating separately or interdependently they serve to yield an apparent motivation to belong (cf. e.g. Festinger, 1950). Though its manifestation is amenable to shaping by the immediate social environment, the component for social approval is doubtless a more stable personal attribute than the motive for a use of the group as a functional instrument, and therefore has features closely akin to what we usually think of as a dimension of personality. With due caution, one could then contend that certain individuals—because of their heightened requirement for social approval as compared with others—are more

[1] This conception is not intended to touch even incidentally upon the issue in psychology of "latent learning." That there are motives underlying the learning of expectancies may be conceded. Moreover, the way in which expectancies fashion behavior is variously documented, as in the experiment on perceived "acceptance" by Dittes and Kelley (1956), and in Julian and Steiner (1961).

likely to "conform" than will these others. But this is by no means a one-to-one proposition, and it assuredly does not operate in reverse. By now I would hope we are agreed that simply identifying evident conformity behavior, by whatever definition, and then inferring from this an individually-centered propensity to conform is a mistake. Other factors come into play, a few of which I have suggested, and some of which are yet to be treated.

The perceptual element in conformity

Conceptions of conformity invariably involve a double assumption: that the individual is aware of some norm (or expectancy), and that his manifest behavior in accord with this standard is indicative of conformity. The prospect of random behavior is usually excluded from concern, and for our purposes, we may simply note this and move to the more substantial issue of perceptual accuracy and inaccuracy in conformity.

Clearly, it is not necessarily true that an individual in any sense "knows" what is expected of him within a given social milieu. In the universe of experience, many cases very likely could be identified where this basal condition is in fact absent. What may then happen depends in some measure upon the motivation of the individual, whatever its source. Should he desire to make a go of it—"play the game," so to speak—he will effectively try hard to find out what is expected; if not motivated, he may not achieve awareness and may be thought to be a boor, or some such, by the relevant others. Still another element may be postulated though, i.e. a factor of general alertness to persons and events in the social realm. Given someone low in this characteristic, it follows that even if highly motivated to do the "right thing," he might fail and thus give evidence of nonconformity. Hence, a person could wish to conform to what others actually expect of him, fall short because of this basic perceptual inadequacy, and so "conform" to an incorrectly perceived standard; he would consequently appear to be nonconforming when, in fact, his motivation, or intent, lay elsewhere.

Status and conformity

In the matter of status, mentioned in an earlier context, we have still another outcome of interaction. People do not, after all, possess status as an immutable personal attribute. It rests foremost in the eyes of one or more perceivers; and, whether directly or indirectly, it is these others who in some sense accord status. To comprehend status, we must therefore look to the differentiated view of one individual held by others, especially since these have certain operational results in their interaction.

Briefly, then, a differentiated perception, with effects upon interpersonal expectancies, conditions a particular behavioral approach to the object person. Since the expectancies applicable to the behavior of this person are in some way special, he is perceived, reacted to, and expected to behave uniquely. Status may thus be considered as some accumulation of positively disposed impressions, residing in the perceptions of relevant others, and having operational significance. This may be conceived to extend along an implicit continuum of esteem.

The genesis of this perceptual differentiation comes about from social interaction, though this does not discount the prospect of a symbolic communication of status. From the past interactions that occur, one individual makes an impression on another. An ongoing record of this interaction thus develops, with consequent expectations regarding this other. Within a group framework, two main dimensions appear to be central to this process: the behavior of the object person in accordance with interpersonal expectancies, and his contribution to group goals. The former aspect represents a recasting of conformity, the latter a recognition of task competence as a distinguishable though commonly related determiner of status.

The scheme amounts very simply to this: as the individual is perceived to behave in accordance with commonly applied expectancies, and makes contributions toward the group's activities, his status moves upward. For convenience, this may be thought of as an accumulation of credits, and, as indicated in Chapter 15, I have specifically affixed to this the term, "idiosyncrasy credit."

Where an individual fails to live up to expectancies, i.e. nonconforms, he loses credits. But, he may maintain some appropriate level of credits by continuing to be perceived as a contributor to the fulfillment of the goals of the group. When an individual's credit balance reaches zero, he may be thought of as having been excluded from the group, so far as the group's perception of him is concerned. On the other hand, credits may accumulate to such a level that the expectancies applicable to the individual are directed toward innovation. The critical feature here is that status will allow greater latitude in the manifestation of behavior which would be seen to be nonconformist for the other members of the group.

For the person who is upwardly mobile, group expectancies will be altered in the fashion indicated. Because of this shift, it becomes increasingly less appropriate for him to continue to manifest behavior which was set to the group's earlier expectancies. To the extent that the "incipient status person" is attuned to these alterations, and is capable of reacting appropriately to them, his status should at least remain fixed, or move upward. Demands for perceptual accuracy and flexibility of behavior are thus continually made upon him—features of informal leadership borne out by a good deal of research and discussed further in Chapter 20.

Since the high status person has latitude for the manifestation of behavior which for others would be seen as nonconformist, he is in a position to alter the common expectancies of the group. It is in this realm that status may be exercised in an influence sense. Still another condition may hold though for expectancies centered in the status itself; the leader could readily lose credits, and find his latitude diminished, if he should violate these. Regarding such deviation, one dimension that is quite probably significant would be the leader's motivation to belong as it is perceived by the members of the group to be both high and sincere. In the absence of these conditions, his status would be threatened.

In sum, conformity serves to maintain or increase status early in interaction, while later, status allows a greater degree of latitude for nonconformity. Though something of an oversimplification, this formulation serves to explain the seeming paradox that the leader both conforms to group norms and yet operates to alter group norms. This, of course, is no paradox at all. In the model of emergent leadership offered here, an individual achieves status by fulfilling common expectancies and demonstrating task competence during his early exposure to a group. As he continues to amass credits he may eventually reach a threshold which permits deviation and innovation, insofar as this is perceived by the others to be in the group's interests. He can then use credits to deviate in certain realms with relative impunity. Experimental findings bearing on this model are presented here in Chapters 17, 18, and 19.

Conformity as a process

In the foregoing, I have sought to argue against the view that conformity is a persisting personal attribute, as in being lame, or even a passing state, as in having a rash. Rather, I have urged a view of conformity as a *process* leading somewhere, a point which is further elaborated in Chapter 16. Moreover, to my view this is both a universal process and one with a significant *raison d'être* in the scheme of human affairs. Without invoking the metaphysical, or trading in the paradoxical, I should like to suggest the prospect that individuals find conformity a device for gaining individuality. In interactions with groups, they are continually bartering one thing for another, even if inadequately and sometimes to their detriment. If we put value judgments aside then, conformity to a socially prescribed pattern, even to a slavish extent, should not lead us to conclude a profound surrender of individuality: we may be too hasty in branding this an overdesire for social approval when it might well be indicative of a form of pretense used to gain acceptance for other, more important, individually based behavior. These purposive features of manifest behavior require additional elucidation and study.

Summary

Social conformity, in the sense of behavior seen to accord with a social norm, has been variously attributed to relatively stable motive patterns of the individual, to a dimension of personality, or to group characteristics.

These conceptions have been examined here taking account of the fundamental problem posed by the very definition of conformity behavior. Thus it was noted that conformity and nonconformity, as regards process, are not necessarily established by the simple criterion of manifest behavior; that conformity must have, at bottom, a basis in a realistic awareness of the norm by the individual actor; and that the notion of a fixed norm is very likely misleading insofar as it may not apply to all individuals comprising the group of reference.

The central thesis developed upon this base is essentially as follows: an individual functions within a social field largely in terms of his perception of the "group expectancies" regarding his behavior. Depending upon motivational and perceptual states, as they relate to certain features of the social field, he will be more or less given to behavior in keeping with these expectancies. Expectancies are not static but rather depend upon the outcome of past interaction between the individual and relevant others. A core element then is the historical or time-linked effects of interaction in determining the countervailing perceptions of the individual and these others. The effects of this stochastic process, especially upon leadership emergence, is developed in Chapter 20.

15

Conformity, status, and idiosyncrasy credit

Something of a paradox exists in the prevailing treatments of conformity and status. Students of social psychology are likely to be left with the pat impression that the freely chosen leader conforms to, and perhaps tenaciously upholds, the norms of his group. Yet this kind of leadership is also presented as a status sufficient to provide latitude for directing and altering group norms (Homans, 1950, p. 416). From their related experimental work in this area, Dittes and Kelley have voiced a doubt that the relationship between conformity and status is ever a simple one (1956, p. 106). The evidence favors their assertion.

Although these phenomena may be treated as discrete entities, they both arise from interaction between an individual and a set of relevant other individuals constituting a group. To say that an individual conforms, or that he has status, is not to say that these are independently determined states nor that they are terminal; they have some common origin in a phenomenal relationship which persists over time. Conformity and status may be thought of therefore as mutually dependent, and transitionally effective upon subsequent interactions. With this as a framework, several

Reprinted from the *Psychological Review*, 1958, 65, 117-127, with permission of the publisher, the American Psychological Association.

general conceptions will be expressed here regarding mechanisms which produce these phenomena and govern their relationship to one another.

In a gross way, three classes of variables, or elements, are necessary to this conceptual scheme: characteristics of the individual himself; characteristics of the group with which he interacts; and outcomes of interaction representing a past history which may alter the relationship of the former elements.

Of particular importance as a mediating process is the changing perception brought about in the individual and the group by their interaction; the third element is, in effect, this process. A distinction is required, therefore, between the phenomenal and perceptual features of behavior. An individual's behavior is not only phenomenally present in interaction but is also subject to view and appraisal by the other members of the group. If there are to be consequences involving these others, it is essential that there be a perceptual intake on their part. And so too must the individual perceive a group norm; the fact that it is manifestly there is not enough.

It is worth emphasizing that the focus here is upon how the individual fares in the group rather than upon more global consequences to the group. Two kinds of interlocking mechanisms are of concern: those giving rise to behavior in conformity with group demands, and those giving rise to status. The issues at stake may be put simply as follows: What produces conformity? And what allows for nonconformity?

Some questions on conformity

Fundamental to these issues is the matter of determining *when* an individual may be said to be conforming. As we have noted, a twofold assumption underpins the usual view of conformity, i.e. that the individual is aware of the existence of a given group norm, and that his behavior in accordance with this norm is evidence of conformity. It is doubtful that both features of this assumption necessarily hold simultaneously. This being so, difficulties of interpretation will arise. If the individual were to be insensitive to the norm he could hardly be said to be conforming to it, whatever his behavior seemed to betray; correspondingly, a kind of "conformity" might prevail in terms of adherence to an incorrectly perceived norm; and thus, an evident failure to conform might or might not be "nonconformity" depending upon the accuracy of the individual's perception of the norm in the first place.

A related question concerns the individual's motivation. Is there a motive for nonconformity identifiable? Insofar as they are distinguishable, is it necessarily so, after all, that a conflict obtains between the individual's dispositions and the group's demands? Since behavior is taken to be more than a random event, the motivation for instances of conformity or nonconformity should be accountable, once the presence of an adequate recognition of the norm is established.

There remains too the question of who perceives a given behavior to be conforming, i.e. an external observer, a group member, or the actor himself. Employing a fixed-norm baseline for observation, as is often done, serves to obscure differential expectations which render conforming behavior for one individual nonconforming for another—with regard, that is, to others' perceptions *in situ*. Thus, the degree of familiarity with the unique properties of the group context is critical in verifying and understanding conformity.

Norms, roles, and group expectancies

The usual conception of conformity examined here requires some group referent and a standard of behavior abstracted therefrom and defined as a norm. Probably because many studies of groups have involved highly manifest behaviors, norms are conceived to be quite literally evident. On the other hand, in the related concept of role a recognition exists that the behavioral standard may not be manifest, but rather may be an *expectancy*.[1]

Though persisting, the distinction between norms and roles is neither essential nor easy to maintain (cf. Newcomb, 1950; Bates, 1956). Roles are normative in that they involve some implicit shared expectancy among group members; and norms themselves, lacking visibility, may nonetheless dwell in expectancies. It is these expectancies, then, which may be normative, in the sense of typicality. Norms and roles are only distinguishable insofar as norms usually imply expectancies applicable to many persons, while roles are expectancies restrictive to one or a very few individuals in a group.

Objective observers might delimit common expectancies appropriate to group members in general from differential expectancies having reference to particular individuals as such. For the individual in the setting, however, manifest conformity probably comes about without regard to a separate awareness of norms as distinct from roles, but more likely in terms of behaviors which he perceives to be expected of him by relevant others, i.e. "doing the *right* thing."

In the world of daily interaction, the perception an individual holds of what relevant others expect of him is a singularly important determinant of his social behavior; and the degree to which an individual perceives the group to be rewarding serves to enhance or elaborate the effect produced by his motivation to belong. An alternative sequence may be seen to occur as well: motivation having reference to some fulfillment through the group serves to heighten the individual's perception of its expectancies.[2]

---

1 The term "expectancy" refers to another's perception of some object person (cf. Steiner, 1955). What the object person then perceives to be the expectancy is quite important, but its locus is first of all in the "other." Reference is not made, therefore, to the term in Tolman's sense.

2 The work on selective perception (e.g. Postman, Bruner & McGinnies, 1948) sustains some such formulation, in general. But the linkage between motivation and perception has considerably greater complexity, as Bruner (1957) has more recently pointed out.

Individual variables

Granted that conformity derives from certain features of individual perception and motivation, it still remains necessary to identify these features more pointedly. In this formulation, there are four such to be noted: perceptual ability (P_a), representing a general alertness to the social stimulus field; perceptual error (P_e), with particular reference to group expectancies; motivation to gain or sustain social approval (M_a); and motivation to take part in the focal activities of the group (M_g). Taken together, the latter two variables may be considered as the individual's motivation to belong to the group (M).

The perceptual variables can readily be related to personality typologies. Many of these, e.g. authoritarianism, rigidity, or empathy, appear to lend themselves to a reduction to perceptual function as a core element (cf. Rokeach, 1948; Adorno, *et al.*, 1950; Bender & Hastorf, 1953). Terms like "perceptual rigidity," "perceptual defense," and "social imperceptiveness," often appear as concomitants of these broader characterizations; evidently, this element accounts for certain diversities in behavior which distinguish individuals from one another.

It is useful here, however, to recognize a differential between that which is given and that which is emergent, i.e. perceptual ability and perceptual error, though the interaction of the two is not challenged. The distinction basically is that the former serves as a parameter setting the lower limit on the latter. Thus, the minimum level of an individual's P_e is set by his basic capacity, P_a. This should not be taken as neglect of the potentials of learning, however. The concept of capacity introduced here may be understood to be similar to that of cognitive structures (cf. Krech, 1951). No assumptions are made about the source of the "capacity"; it is only significant as a feature of the individual which bears upon interaction. It seems reasonable to believe that some individuals have an initial advantage over others as regards accuracy in perceiving group expectancies.

Concerning motivation to belong, mention has already been made that it involves two continua: motivation specific to the activity—or instrumental features—of the group, M_g; and motivation rooted in a generalized need for social approval, M_a. This view cuts across a number of other motivational schema suggested elsewhere (cf. Festinger, 1950; Bovard, 1953; Deutsch & Gerard, 1955; Jackson & Saltzstein, 1956; Thibaut & Strickland, 1956), and is intended more as a resolution than a departure. Briefly, these other distinctions appear to involve an "activity focus" and an "other people focus." Activity involves others, of course, but not necessarily to gain their approval. What really seems to matter is the nature of the reward sought.

The approval variable might be viewed as a parameter of personality, but not one so static as to be unaffected by interaction, within certain limits. Since those members having interests which can only be satisfied through participation in group activity do not of necessity have a high need for social approval, and since those cast into groups of little positive activity valence to them may still require approval, it is possible that these variables may be related negatively or positively, depending upon the circumstances considered.

Status emergence

The foregoing points have concentrated on individual characteristics that absorb and deal with features of the social context. Ultimately, these have consequences in behavior, which in its turn has an impact upon the group. It is appropriate now to consider the implications of this process to the emergence of status.

At bottom, status may be taken to be an outcome of the group's differentiated perception of the individual, leading to a set of particularized expectancies regarding his behavior. This occurs as a function of certain of the behaviors or characteristics evidenced by the individual in interaction, which then yield a reconstruction of the group's perception of him. Cast in these terms, status has special value as a kind of middle ground in relating the individual to the group. It exists in the first place as a feature in someone's perceptual field, for without reference to a perceiver status has no intrinsic value or meaning in itself. And, similarly, role cannot be divorced from its perceptual locus; behavior is only appropriate to status insofar as someone perceives it to be so. Perceptual differentiation by the group has consequences, then, in terms of the behaviors it expects the individual to display.[3]

Though not necessarily the case, it is desirable to conceive of status within this framework as having hierarchical properties on some sort of group-acceptance continuum (cf. Dittes & Kelley, 1956). This is by no means critical as a feature, but is of heuristic value. Still further, it is convenient to represent status as permitting greater latitude in the manifestation of behaviors which would be seen to be nonconformist for the other members of the group; we refer here to common expectancies, a term introduced earlier. The implications of this aspect of status are of especial relevance to what follows.

Idiosyncrasy credit

Status will hereafter be considered to be an outcome of interaction referred to as "idiosyncrasy credit" (C). This represents an accumulation of positively disposed impressions residing in the perceptions of relevant others; it is defined operationally in terms of the degree to which an individual may deviate from the common expectancies of the group. In this view, each individual within a group—disregarding size and function, for the moment—may be thought of as having a degree of group-awarded credits such as to permit idiosyncratic behavior in certain dimensions *before* group sanctions are applied. By definition, affiliation with the group—as

[3] Implicit here is a concern with observable features of the individual. Thus, in the case of conformity, public manifestation is required; another position, taking account of both public and private conformity, has been advanced by Jahoda (1959).

perceived by the group—ceases when the individual's credit balance reaches zero.

It is noteworthy that this concept is applicable to the limited, artificially produced laboratory group as well as to the total society. And, since the individual may have simultaneous membership in many groups, he may be considered to have a distinct credit balance in all groups with which he is in some sense involved; in each case he has achieved some level of status. Affixed to this concept of "credit" is the further consideration that "debits" of varying magnitudes may be charged against the credit balance, depending upon the gravity and frequency of the idiosyncrasy manifested, and the credit level which the individual holds.[4]

Taking our society today as an illustration, one's credit balance very likely will be rapidly exhausted by publicly espousing Communist doctrine. In a different sphere, a fraternity man may experience comparable rejection by his peers for growing a beard, though other factors would come into play, so that for some individuals the consequences—in terms of group sanctions—would be disastrous and for others hardly disturbing. This requires some consideration of factors which determine the awarding of credit.

Among other determinants, the credit balance that a group member achieves depends upon the group, its function, and other properties to be considered below. It is useful for our purposes here to conceive of an "open system," i.e. an autonomous group providing focal activities, as well as free face-to-face interaction yielding expectancies; this would permit the simultaneous observation of an individual's behavior by all group members and the generation of impressions representing credit.

There are three general variables which can be delineated as determinants of these impressions. The first of these is alpha value (V_a), referring to the individual's task competence or perform-

---

[4] Alterations upward or downward in credit may be conceived as a negative, monotonic function of credit balance. Thus, for the same idiosyncratic behavior or negative weight attached to value, the individual with high status loses less credit than the marginal individual of low status (cf. Schachter, 1951).

ance in regard to focal group activities; the second is beta value (V_β), referring to characteristics of the individual not specific to these activities, e.g. status in a broader group, *bonhomie*, and the like; the third is immediate past idiosyncratic behavior (B), constituting a drain on credits.[5] It is not contended that credit is necessarily related linearly to these variables, nor is their very likely interrelationship ignored. They are doubtless intercorrelated, though of varying degrees of significance in generating or dissipating credits. As a generalization, value (V) tends to increase credit while idiosyncratic behavior (B) acts to decrease credit—though the potential for negative value exists, e.g. in the case of prejudice.

Group variables

From the foregoing it should be apparent that an individual can only be accurate in perceiving expectancies insofar as they are normative, in some modal sense, and are communicated. Two interrelated group variables which have importance in this regard are group attraction (A) and the communicality of any given expectancy (Y).

The former variable may be thought of as "cohesiveness," a term more usually applied. But since this term may have at least several operational meanings, it is preferable to specify two kinds of literal attraction, or an aggregation of these: attraction to group members, and attraction to focal group activities. This duality follows the M_a and M_g distinction made earlier in connection with motivation to belong. Although one may deal with a nondiscriminate aggregation of these, it is quite true that the sum of individual attractions in the group may be based predominately in M_a needs

[5] Still another variable related to credit balance, probably curvilinearly, would be the duration of the individual's affiliation with the group over time. This has been disregarded, since it is useful to deal with individuals as though they have been in the group for an equal period of time, more particularly from its inception. It is also likely that the degree to which the individual is "visible" may alter the effects produced by his value and idiosyncratic behavior.

or M_g needs, and that differences in the emergent characteristics of groups thus constituted will be evident. Thus, where group attraction derives mainly from M_a one might predict it would be more stable than where its source is mainly M_g, since the latter variable is more temporally based.

Communicality is conceived to be directly related to group attraction in a mutual dependency; it refers to the degree to which an expectancy is literally communicated, i.e. made evident, and bears a relationship to both relevance and communication variables, as they have been introduced in other formulations (cf. Chowdhry & Newcomb, 1952; Talland, 1954), though this is by no means a complete statement. Studies of leaders' ability to estimate group attitudes, for example, have yielded highly conflicting results (cf. Steiner, 1955, p. 268). Where attitudes are "relevant," leaders *may* or *may not* be superior to nonleaders in their respective estimates; where leaders *are* found to be superior to nonleaders in estimating relevant attitudes, this has been ascribed to the heightened social sensitivity of leaders or alternatively to the proposition that leaders are instrumental in the shaping of group attitudes and hence tend to know them better.

Whatever the explanation chosen, there is reason to contend that the variable of relevance may not be the most fruitful one for purposes of study. If one were disposed to test the tenability of the hypothesis that leaders have this greater social sensitivity it would seem desirable not only to raise the question of whether leaders, and others, tend to use their own personal attitudes as an anchorage for estimating group attitudes, but to ask in addition whether this exists independently of the degree to which given attitudes actually are foci of communication within real groups. Another approach, accordingly, might be to utilize some index of the degree to which a specific attitude—or an expectancy—actually evidences itself in a given group. There is utility, then, in introducing the operationalizable property "communicality."

Though a level of communicality may characterize a group, the particular center of interest here resides in a given expectancy. On

may venture in this vein that the communicality of an expectancy
will be at a lower relative level than that of other expectancies, if it
is less applicable to the group as a whole; common expectancies
ought to have higher communicality than the differential expectancies associated with increased status. Since communicality rests
on behavior, it may be seen to follow, too, that interpersonal interaction results in higher communicality. Through a related mecha-
nism, interpersonal interaction may contribute to group attraction
(cf. Homans, 1950; Newcomb, 1956).

Summary of variables

For convenience, the variables described may now be set forth
definitionally.

B—*Idiosyncratic behavior*, i.e. any group member's behavior
which may be perceived by the group to deviate from a given group
expectancy.

C—*Idiosyncrasy credit*, i.e. the extent to which a given group
member's idiosyncratic behavior (B) is allowable, in terms of
gravity and frequency, before group sanctions are applied.

V_a—*Alpha value*, i.e. the weight assigned the current performance of a given individual, which may be perceived by the group
as bearing upon its focal activities, e.g. task competence.

V_β—*Beta value*, i.e. the weight assigned the characteristics of a
given individual which may be perceived by the group, but are not
specific to its current focal activities, e.g. status external to the
group.

P_a—The *perceptual ability* of a given individual, in the sense of
a capacity to perceive events and relationships in the social field.

P_e—The *perceptual error* of a given individual in perceiving
events or relationships in a particular social field, e.g. group expectancies.

M_a—The *motivation* of a given individual to affiliate with a
given group, in terms of gaining or sustaining *social approval*.

M_g—The *motivation* of a given individual to affiliate with a group, in terms of interest in focal *group activity*.

M—*Individual motivation to gain or sustain membership*, i.e. some composite of a given individual's motivation of both the M_a and M_g variety.

A—In general, *attraction of the group to its members*, i.e. some aggregate of all group members' M.

Y—The *communicality of a given group expectancy*, in terms of the degree to which a given expectancy is evident.

Schematic representation

In Fig. 1 our symbolic notation has been employed to represent relationships schematically. Since a sequential pattern is of particular importance, a time dimension is involved throughout; thus, subscripts are introduced to indicate the time interval to which reference is made; e.g. t_1 is read as the first time interval; or, P_{e2} as perceptual error in the second time interval.

The system originates at the top with group attraction as a motivational context, and three individual variables, perceptual ability, motivation to gain or sustain social approval, and motivation with reference to the group's activity. At the next level, group attraction has given rise to the communicality of certain expectancies which are then perceived by the individual, thus yielding a perceptual error; and motivation to belong has been aggregated at this level, as well. Beta value is also introduced to signify the group's perception of the individual's characteristics, e.g. pleasant appearance.[6]

Moving down in time, the individual's idiosyncratic behavior during the period just elapsed has been generated by his error in

[6] The term "group perception" refers to an abstraction; it is unlikely that all members of a group will perceive a given feature of an individual identically; the intent therefore is only to suggest a modal tendency. However, some quite pertinent research has illuminated this point and given credence to the general conception of differentially-determined value (cf. Jones & deCharms, 1957).

perceiving expectancies together with his motivation—within the constraints imposed by the level of group attraction. The group's perception of the individual's contribution to its focal activities, alpha value, is influenced by the immediately prior perception of his characteristics, beta value.

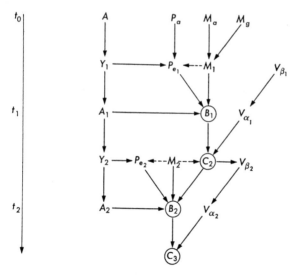

Fig. 1. Schematic representation of mechanisms demonstrating relationships over time.

In the next stage, status is generated—in the form of group-awarded credits—by the effects of behavior relative to expectancies and the sequence of beta value to alpha value to credits. At this point the full set of interactions are in play, with credits affecting beta value, the latter serving as a repository of group perceptions of the individual's characteristics; perceptual error and motivation are reintroduced for this new phase, with the former affected by communicality of expectancies. Idiosyncratic behavior is subsequently determined by available credits, as this is checked by motivation, in particular, and perceptual error.

Discussion and implications

Early in interaction, conformity to group expectancies serves to
maintain or increase status, particularly as it is seen to be combined with manifest contributions to the group; at a later phase,
however, the status thus generated permits greater latitude for
idiosyncratic behavior. Thus, if an individual conforms to expectancies early in his exposure to the group and if he shows characteristics of competence, he accrues credits. For evident deviations
from expectancies, or poor performance, he loses credits. If he ex-
hausts his credit balance completely, pressures are applied to
remove him from the group, or, at the very least, he is no longer
perceived to be a member. At the other pole, if he continues to
amass credits he attains a threshold permitting deviations from
common expectancies, but with constraints imposed by newly
differentiated expectancies.

The apparent paradox—that leaders both conform to group
norms and yet may act to alter them by an exercise of influence—
may be explained by reference to this sequential process. In this
regard, it should not be supposed that an abundance of credits
must lead perforce to influence. While an individual thus endowed
has the potential to display more idiosyncratic behavior than others,
he might not do so, nor would he of necessity become a leader
thereby. Some further points of clarification are in order.

It is easy enough for the individual to continue to do habitually
that which is rewarded by relevant others, so long as expectancies
remain relatively stable. Consider the state of affairs which holds,
however, in the case of the person who has marked status mobility
in the group. He cannot simply continue to redisplay behaviors
which were appropriate to the group's earlier expectancies, because
the expectancies applicable to him are now altered in keeping with
his rising status. Other things being equal, this suggests two features appropriate to the attainment of status in an open system:
(a) accuracy of social perception; and (b) modifiability of behavior. Insofar as the incipient status person is attuned to the

altering group expectancies and is capable of reacting appropriately to them, his status will very likely move upward. The relationship of these points to research on leadership is noteworthy; for example, the proposition that leaders have a heightened sensitivity to certain properties of the social context is in consonance with the foregoing. Note, too, that whether or not the leader has actually created a feature of the context with which he is then familiar, he may well have evidenced perceptual accuracy in an earlier phase, as he rose to leadership. Accordingly, the finding of Talland (1954) that leaders are only better in judging norms where they have had a part in their evolution is not inconsistent with a finding like that of Chowdhry and Newcomb (1952) to the effect that leaders have superior social perception; it would appear that the time phase under study is critical in yielding one process or the other.

Previously the point was made that the high-status person could effect changes in the common expectancies of the group because he has latitude for the manifestation of what would be seen to be nonconforming behavior for others. But, in contrast, the expectancies regarding the role itself are less amenable to alteration by the incumbent. Hence, the leader could readily lose credits and find his influence diminished if he were to show idiosyncratic behavior in terms of expectancies associated with his role. Regarding such deviation, we may conceive of one requirement which is quite likely significant, i.e. perception by the members of the group that the leader's motivation to belong be both high and sincere. Should this condition not be fulfilled, status may be threatened. To take another illustration, innovation by the leader may be of high valence to the group. It is conceivable that this could yield the seeming anomaly of a leader who, in the face of this expectancy, adopts a passive and ostensibly safe course, but loses status.

Leadership status, therefore, assuredly demands conformity to the group's expectancies regarding the role, but still leaves the leader with sway in the sphere of common expectancies associated with members at large. The leader may deviate from these, or bring about their reconstruction, if his prior activities have generated an appropriately high level of credit.

The motivational aspects of this process require consideration in terms of the individual set against the background of the group's activity. The restraining effect of M on the expenditure of C has been accounted for in the foregoing. What is more to the point, however, is the fact that a person with M_g will more likely achieve status in a largely M_g group than will a person with M_a; the status achieved, therefore, is a part function of the congruence of the individual's motivation with the generalized character of the motivation extant in the group. Since motivation is related, as well, to performance and other characteristics represented by alpha value and beta value, it is to be regarded as a key element.

If the group has a primary focal activity, then presumably M_g becomes more highly valued, particularly in combination with alpha value. At the other extreme, i.e. where the group activities are quite diffuse, M_a becomes important in combination with beta value. We may conceptualize groups of the M_a variety as being essentially "socially minded." With a minimum group-centered function requiring broad participation, the person having beta value is more likely to achieve status through being well liked; in the M_g group, to the contrary, alpha value becomes critical and task competence has greater weight in determining status. The relationship of this to the current situational view of leadership is evident.[7]

Whether group members do distinguish between value of one kind or another can be inferred from the literature of sociometry. Evidence will be found there indicating that individuals can give scaled evaluations of their peers with quite adequate discriminations between those they like, those they consider competent, and so forth. Though these sociometrically based status continua are likely to be related, as we have previously noted, they are by no

[7] For example, the finding of Jennings (1950) that leadership and popularity are highly related in her groups can be considered in this framework.

means in universal, one-to-one correspondence (cf. Hollander & Webb, 1955). Viewing status in the aggregative, credit-amassing sense still allows for the integrity of the roots which feed it. Experimental evidence on the basis for shifts in the group's perception of a member also accords with this conception (cf. Jones & deCharms, 1957).

Certain of the assumptions made here—e.g. that an individual will have a level of credit reposing unitarily in others' perceptions of him, and that he may know and make use of the credits at his disposal—are only approximations of reality. Their literal tenability is not, however, crucial to the mechanisms postulated. One could argue that the individual operates *as if* these assumptions were in fact true: the "they" commonly invoked to denote the upholders of some social pattern are never quite as homogeneous as the term suggests; but, to the individual, the use of "they" to represent a supposed uniformity is a necessary convenience as a basis for behavior. Furthermore, in accordance with this position, the individual apparently does react differentially to what he believes to be the view of him held by the "they," as Dittes and Kelley (1956) have demonstrated by manipulating the level of group "acceptance" which an individual is permitted to sense. In general, then, it appears that the individual seeks to know where he stands and does the best he can with the information available to him. These conceptions therefore do no violence to the reality with which the individual deals, but rather describe this reality in terms congruent with his concern.

Summary

Beginning with the consideration that social behavior depends upon attributes of the individual, conditions of the situation, and inputs to a dynamic system arising from their interaction, a theoretical conception relating conformity and status is presented.

The major mediating construct introduced is "idiosyncrasy credit," taken to be an index of status, in the operational sense of permitting deviations from common "expectancies" of the group.

Credits are postulated to increase or decrease as a function of the group's perception of the individual's task performance and generalized characteristics, and of his "idiosyncratic behavior," i.e. deviations from its expectancies. Though increases in credit are seen to permit greater latitude for idiosyncratic behavior, motivational and perceptual states of the individual, and group-level phenomena, are also considered.

16

Reconsidering the issue of conformity
in personality

Quite oblivious to the notions we may have about the categorization of behavior, people nonetheless persist in behaving. So it is that we observe some manner of behavior and call it "conformity," and so it is that we may at times attribute this to something we choose to call "personality."

In my comments here, I hope to examine this latter conception in light of certain points adduced from social psychology. Thus, in anticipation of what is to come, conformity, whatever else it may be, constitutes a problem of person perception, and for a set of reasons which I shall dwell upon later. But, by way of beginning, we might now give first consideration to personality as a construct.

The manifest and the underlying in personality

The issue of whether to deal with the manifest or the underlying strikes deeply at the roots of modern psychology. Far from withering, this dualism is more full-bodied than ever, and nowhere more

Adapted from Chapter 11 in Henry P. David and J. C. Brengelmann (Eds.), *Perspectives in Personality Research*, New York, Springer Publishing Co., copyright © 1960. Reprinted by permission of the publisher.

so than in our conception of personality. Reflecting this, we have as an example Nevitt Sanford's ranging presentation (1956). He offers a not unorthodox view of personality with levels of "depth" such that some attributes of the individual are more basic than others, and hence accessible only through the most penetrating study.

What continues to perplex, however, is the linkage between these underlying features and the overt behaviors which are observed. Are these related? And, if so, by what mechanisms do the former mediate their influence to the latter? What of behaviors at the "surface" which appear to have little relevance to the "core"? May we accept these as in some way indicative of the nature of that core? Granted that this is possible, when are we entitled to make such inferences? Taking Sanford literally, it would seem that we can't be sure, for he suggests that the "core" be given over to study by "personologists" and that the "surface" be delivered up to further study by the social psychologist.

To the social psychologist this can only serve to compound confusion. If he is to be concerned with the individual, it must be in terms of those attributes—or "things about an individual"— which may be stably related to some palpable social behaviors. As matters now stand, there *is* precisely such a line of interest which has given rise to a multitude of attitudinally based trait scales geared to the measurement of dispositions (e.g. authoritarianism, rigidity, empathy) presumed to be generators of characteristic social behavior. In fact, this represents a concern with that which is underlying—call it core or what you will.

But side by side with this stream of activity in social psychology, and flourishing with relative independence, is yet another stream. This is represented in the work of the situational determinists who focus particular attention upon the immediate situation, particularly group influences, in eliciting social behavior. Here individual characteristics are mainly taken as parameters which are given; there is, therefore, no singular handling of the individual *qua* individual.

Accordingly, we are in the first place beset with a twofold view of personality: as an underlying individual attribute bringing about behavior, and as a literal set of behaviors typically displayed by the individual, other things being equal. We are committed, furthermore, to a conception of behavior as having some relevance to the nature of situational forces acting upon the individual. There is no royal road to understanding in either of these approaches alone. It seems reasonable to suppose that there are not only individual differences in disposition toward certain behaviors, but that there also exist situationally determined variants of behavior among individuals. How these two lines of influence may interact to yield some vector of behavior remains a focal point of concern, and one that will occupy our attention at greater length later. For the logic of what is to come, it is worthwhile briefly to draw an analogy with the experience of chemistry.

The "Essence" pitfall

The behavior of matter has a tradition of speculation which may even antedate that of primitive psychology. In the antiquity of chemistry, phenomena were noted and accounted for with reference to certain essences presumed to inhere in the substance; a given manifest property carried the imputation of its essence to the bit of matter being observed. Essences were catalogued at length in an attempt to establish causal relationships. But rather static qualities (like hardness, coldness, or dampness) were typically fixed upon and these proved quite inadequate as a foundation for a science of chemistry.

Substantial breakthroughs did not occur until the age of Boyle, Lavoisier, and Dalton, among others, when the relevant properties of a substance were recognized to be those which were affected by combination with other substances under varying conditions of exposure. The consequences of this then new view require no embellishment. Close upon the realization that *interactive* attributes were critical, rather than static features, there evolved the law of conservation of mass, the kinetic theory of gases, nine-teenth-century atomic theory, and ultimately the periodic table of elements.

Analogies may be overdrawn, and I too share a disdain for invidious comparisons with the physical sciences, as though what suits them must necessarily suit us. Yet, I have set down this particular parallel because, rough as it may be, it affords a fresh opportunity to consider some of the rubrics to which we are beholden. Thus, I submit that even with our sophistication in measurement, we are still inclined to search for those characteristics of the individual—his essences—which might account for behavior and hence be worthy of heroic feats of dimensionalization. Largely through the instrumentality of the personality test—or the F Scale, the Water Jar Problem, the Test of Empathy, and so forth—we have hopefully tapped some of these already.

In this process, though, I believe that we have failed to recognize the two-pronged conception of personality we hold. And, more to the point, we may gloss over the likely fact that both prongs obscure or subsume interactive properties of the individual which require for their elicitation certain catalytic situational elements. Too often, on the contrary, we choose to deal with them as static attributes, having a level of consistency over time which is probably quite unrealistic.

Thus it is not surprising that in a literature coverage McClelland (1956) has commented that "the best conclusion one can draw seems to be that the status of rigidity as a trait variable is, to say the least, uncertain!" We may note, as another case in point, that the F Scale bears a highly varying relationship to behaviors as the situational context is varied (cf. Titus & Hollander, 1957). This is not to be taken as a dismissal of this approach, however. Rather, I would suggest that we recognize its limitations as regards prediction over many situations; its fulfillment rests on a study of those relevant situational catalysts noted earlier.

Social conformity as an outcome

How the foregoing points bear upon contemporary concerns in social psychology may be better discerned through consideration of social conformity which, to my mind, constitutes the central process of social psychology—and my particular use of the word "process" is not a matter of indifference. Our interest will cover both illustrative empirical works and some related operational problems.

It is hardly news to suggest that conformity involves an individual in a situation; that is to say, it emerges from interaction. On his own terms, virtually everyone concerned with the problem will grant this as a commonplace truth. But, this widespread acknowledgment notwithstanding, we are still confronted with a persisting treatment of conformity as if it were a function of either the individual or the situation operating unilaterally.

To illuminate this issue, it is convenient to begin with reference to the well-known work on conformity by Crutchfield (1955), taking it as illustrative of a class. The features of the experimental arrangement are by now quite familiar and grow out of some earlier work by Asch (1951). In this experimentally induced group atmosphere, the findings indicate that some subjects will characteristically conform to the norm of the group—that is, give the same response that four other subjects have given—even in the face of rather clear evidence of the group's error. From this the point is adduced that such individuals have an essentially conformist personality, and Crutchfield provides personality assessment data which appear to demonstrate the presence of correlates of conformity in other personality trait dimensions.

There are several points we might now pose about the intended sense in which the term "personality" is used here. Are these *behaviors* personality? Or does personality *determine* the behaviors? If typical behaviors are meant, clearly the sample of situations studied is exceedingly small. Hence, it would seem that the "essence" definition is implied: presumably, people have been identified who are programmed, in some underlying sense, to conform; or are they?

Let it be noted hastily that the Asch-Crutchfield studies are not being indicted, but rather the particular construction put upon their meaning. The confounding element in this picture is that conformity has been imputed to the individual from manifest behavior in this particular situational field; to then speak of conformity as an underlying attribute of the individual himself is questionable since situations vary in their properties, e.g. groups differ in their demands upon individuals, and individuals are variously motivated to respond to these demands. Moreover, we may wonder whether this ostensible conformity response was indeed prompted by motivation to comply with group demands. One might argue with reason that another motive might have been a desire to please the experimenter who, after all, represented an authority figure. Or, perhaps, subjects who "conformed" possessed a low frustration threshold and were negatively motivated, in the sense of wishing to get on with the task so as to escape from the field to some other activity. We may not be sure of their actual impact, but these factors are certainly within the realm of possible effectiveness.

There is yet another point at stake; it is dubious for us to invoke conformity as an individually centered variable (much as pleasure or selfishness were invoked in the days of philosophical conjecture) for the simple reason that it is too gross. Thus, if we say that an individual is a "conformist," in the pervasive, personality "core" sense, we run the risk, other issues aside, of obscuring the dynamic aspects of interaction yielding this evident outcome.

We have a particularly pointed case of the pitfalls of this conception of conformity in Bernberg's (1955) "test of social conformity." His rationale is as follows: people who are nonconformists will get into difficulty with social conventions; those who are conformists will comply with these conventions, as for example in the matter of religious observance. Consequently, he has taken a set of attitude items and validated them as indices of conformity vs. nonconformity by noting their discrimination between church-goers and prisoners, respectively. We are then asked to accept his ultimate scale as a measure of tendencies toward conformity. I, for one, should not be at all surprised to find that jailed prisoners are, shall we say, more antagonistic to social conventions than are church-goers—even though they might themselves have been avid church-goers at one time. But I doubt that this necessarily demonstrates any profound personality disposition toward nonconformity, unless we define conformity as an absence of overtly hostile attitudes toward the very broadest social forms. Again, the omission of a manageable situational referent is damaging to the validity of the claim advanced.

Some points of definition

Rather than prolong this critique, I should now like to lay the groundwork for another approach to conformity as a process leading somewhere. It is a set of behaviors, displayed in a given situation, evidently in keeping with certain demands of the social situation; but nevertheless these are tied to impelling individual motivations and perceptions.

Consider the oft-noted case of uniformity in executive attire. Granted that this can be taken as conformity to a socially prescribed pattern of dress, I would still wish to know what motivates a given person to manifest this fashion. Is it, as we are perhaps too hastily given to conclude, just a desire for social approval? Or is it perhaps a convenient device for being readily accepted, at least superficially, so that then other, more important kinds of behavior become acceptable? Would a young executive, hoping to put across a new advertising campaign, approach his superiors or clients with a boldly checked suit so as to engender a likely perceptual block to the more important commodity he wishes to market, namely an idea? I doubt it.

Nor do I think that the political demagogue who goes into the farm country and snaps his suspenders, chews tobacco, and speaks with the tones of a farm hand, behaves as he does because he is a "conformist personality" desiring social approbation. This is patently absurd. The man wishes to create an impression, an aura, which will smooth the way for his attainment of more important personal goals such as political power. Every successful demagogue must know this implicitly.

There are some other intricacies of definition which should not escape attention. Most basic is the matter of determining *when* an individual may be said to be conforming; and this is a highly relative, rather than absolute, matter. To really distinguish conformity from nonconformity, we ought to be able to distinguish between an individual's very own dispositions and the social demands to which he is subject, something we cannot too readily accomplish now. But suppose, illustratively, we happen to know these are quite in accord. This would suggest that the *appearance* of acquiescing to social demands is not by any means a sure index of conformity. It is also true that without the individual's awareness of social demands, even his apparent acquiescence to them is really not conformity at all; he may be responding quite randomly to a situation he understands only meagerly, yet his behavior, by chance, fits the prescribed pattern.

PERCEPTUAL AND MOTIVATIONAL COMPONENTS

In briefest terms, then, we have said that a twofold assumption tends to pervade our usual conception of conformity: that the individual is aware of the existence of a given group norm, and that his manifest behavior in concordance with this norm is evidence of conformity. It is doubtful that both features of this assumption necessarily hold simultaneously. And this being so, difficulties of interpretation of behavior must necessarily arise.

Therefore, as previously noted, an individual insensitive to a norm could hardly be said to be conforming to it, whatever his behavior *seemed* to betray; correspondingly, a kind of inverse "conformity" might prevail all around us in the form of adherence to a faultily perceived norm. Thus an evident failure to conform might or might not be "nonconformity" depending upon the accuracy of the individual's perception of the norm in the first place.

Returning to the matter of motivation, we would be remiss, I believe, to accept nonconformity at its face value without seeking some motive for its manifestation. Leaving aside the perceptual point noted, we must surely recognize that some individuals might quite freely nonconform because they are motivated to achieve some goal of singular importance, and—what is more significant perhaps—because they know that their status in the particular group context will permit this degree of nonconformity. I do not mean to suggest that all such behavior is reasoned, in the cognitive sense, but I do propose that some individuals may rationally weigh their acceptable range of nonconformity and balance this with the strength of their motive to achieve something personally.

This suggests, as well, the likelihood that conformity is only approximately measured, at best, by the kind of fixed-norm baseline we normally employ. It is possible, indeed highly probable, that conforming behavior for one individual may be nonconforming for another, in terms of the perceptions of group members in the situation. The question of who defines conformity should not be lightly dismissed; I think it matters a great deal whether this is done by the actor himself, by an external observer, or by a fellow group member. The differential expectations in a group, regarding the behavior of individuals in that group, are of more importance than the attention they have received would indicate.

PERSON PERCEPTION FROM INTERACTION

Interaction between an individual and other individuals consists of a good deal more than manifest behaviors. There is a rich current of countervailing perceptions which evolve over time and constitute a past history affecting future interactions. Thus, as I have pointed out at much greater length elsewhere (Hollander, 1958), the individual in a group setting reacts not only in terms of immediate reality, but also in terms of his previously determined perception of the "group expectancies" relevant to his behaviors. These may be in the nature of what we usually think of as "norms" and "roles." And it is also correspondingly the case that his manifest behavior is appraised by other group members in terms of the past history of interaction and their perception of what is appropriate behavior for him.

Consequently, in the case of leadership as representative of a high status in a group, I have argued that a greater latitude is provided for nonconformity in certain realms of behavior since, through past interaction, the leader has accumulated a reservoir of positively disposed impressions among his group members. I call these "idiosyncrasy credits," and take the view that, while an individual may find it necessary to conform to common group expectancies as he rises to the status of leadership, he may be expected to innovate (and thus, in some sense, nonconform) as a function of his achieved status. Early in interaction, then, conformity serves to maintain or increase status, in combination with some manifest contributions to the group; later, however, status allows a greater degree of latitude for nonconformity (see Chapter 15 above).

Interaction does not stand still. There are time-linked variations in the requirements of leadership, at least partly, because perceptions are altered as an individual displays behavior to relevant others over time. Moreover, whether an individual conforms has some anchorage in whether he has previously conformed, and what effects this had elicited from relevant others. Conformity therefore becomes an inextricable part of the pattern of past interactions and accompanying shifts in perception. A "standard of behavior" must therefore be a highly transitory, relative affair.

Individual motivation in conformity

So much for the arena of conformity, and its dynamic, viewed broadly. Let us now consider the particulars of the dynamic. While I have taken exception to any conception of conformity as an individual attribute, I have nonetheless noted the significant role of individual motivation and perception. Thus, the entire position presented here is predicated on the assumption that some impelling force, presumably motivational, operates upon the individual so that he remains in the group; that is to say, the assumption that he is attracted to the group and that he proposes to persist in "playing the game." It is rare indeed to have the argument advanced that this is a linear dimension, although Bovard (1953) has taken precisely this stand in group research which yielded no relationship between conformity and attraction to the group, measured linearly. If for no other reason, this grossness leaves his findings open to question. It is not that these variables need necessarily be related in every corner of the universe of group situations, but rather that at least two kinds of things seem to be involved in attraction to the group.

In the first place, an individual may be motivated to take part in group activity for its own sake, something akin to what Festinger (1950) has suggested as the "instrumental" use of the group. But, as the second point, it is possible for an individual to be motivated by a desire to gain or sustain social approval. These categories are not offered as mutually exclusive. Viewed at the extremes, however, it may be that an individual has interests which require group activity for their satisfaction, with no great concern on his part to secure social approval from the group, along the way; alternatively, another individual might be cast into a group with little positive activity valence for him, yet he may be motivated to do his part out of a desire for social approval.

Whether these variables, illustrative of two likely dimensions of attraction to the group, will be related positively, negatively, or not at all, will of course depend upon the unique features of the individual and group setting involved. The key point, though, is that the motive for gaining social approval is probably relatively less subject to situational variations than the other motive, and may therefore constitute a somewhat more stable attribute in the nature of an individual parameter.

Notice that this is not an assertion that an individual with this attribute will necessarily conform, in any sense of regularity across situations; by now, hopefully, we have contributed to the rejection of such a simplex view. However, taking Sears's (1951) view of personality as "a potential for activity"—and adding that it is realized in certain of a person's perceptual and motivational states— one could make a probability statement which more or less affirms this as a possibility. Some people, to a degree more than others, are reinforced by some manner of social approval; on a *ceteris paribus* basis, therefore, they will strive more than others to obtain such approval. But this does not dictate conformity, in any one-to-one fashion, because of at least one important intervening element, perceptual functioning, to which we now turn special attention.

Individual perception in conformity

In viewing perceptual functioning in relationship to conformity, rather different and often difficult problems are confronted. Among other things, if we conceive of this at bottom as a relatively stable attribute of the individual, we are likely to find that it bears a decidedly nonlinear correspondence with behavior which we may take as indicative of conformity. The reasons for this assertion have been pointed up in the preceding chapter in connection with a perceptual alertness capacity. We need make no assumptions about the source of this capacity; it is only important for our purposes as a feature of the individual which bears upon his interaction with others. It follows then that some individuals have an initial advantage over others in accurately perceiving group expectancies.

Holding situational characteristics and motivational influences constant, we expect that some individuals will more readily perceive the demands of the social context. Thus, it might be that an individual with a limited capacity will be given to more inaccuracies of perception, and hence may "nonconform" more than would an individual with greater capacity. But, on the other hand, with greater alertness to the group expectancies, an individual may more successfully adapt his behavior to their changing course over time. Limited capacity would imply a fixity, or rigidity, if you will, in responding. Though it would not necessarily be apparent, this kind of person might be "conforming" but, in keeping with an observation offered here earlier, to an *incorrectly* perceived expectancy.

This suggests that manifest nonconformity could arise from either a very high perceptual capacity, where the individual appropriately uses the "credits" at his disposal, or from a very low perceptual capacity, where the individual misreads the expectancies and his related availability of "credits."

Though advanced speculatively, this prospect both accounts for, and accords well with, what we know empirically of certain of the personality typologies studied of late in social psychology. The bulk of these, e.g. authoritarianism, rigidity, empathy, center in a perceptual functioning factor as a core element. (See Adorno, *et al.*, 1950; Rokeach, 1948; Bender & Hastorf, 1953.) While one might be reluctant to accept this as a direct well-spring of conformity behavior, it is likely—again, in probability terms—that such behavior has a linkage to relatively stable perceptual states of the individual.

Limitations in prediction

By the foregoing, I have sought to convey the view that there exist individually based correlates of conformity behavior, operating within certain limits. These are not to be considered as giving rise to linear relationships, however. To the contrary, they must be understood to be subtly related to one another, and complexly, and oftentimes perhaps discontinuously, related to conformity. Predicting from them alone is bound to prove inadequate.

Conformity behavior does not lend itself to segmental treatment as either a feature of these individual attributes—personality, if you like—or of the situational field in which the individual is immersed. It would seem rather to be a combined function of prevailing situational conditions and stable states which are likely to yield certain behavioral outcomes, at times in accordance with more or less explicit expectancies of relevant others. The ongoing nature of this interactive process, with related perceptual changes occurring in the actor and the relevant others, has significant consequences as well.

Research implications

Threading through these comments are signposts aimed at research to be done, and new relationships to be explored. What we appear to require basally is a more rigorous specification of both the dynamic and operational dimensions of conformity. Our criterion, repeatedly challenged here, suffers from an undue acceptance of the superficial at its face value. To observe only the manifest, and then make inferences about the underlying, is to run profound risks of misinterpretation. It is no simple task to tap the motivational and perceptual innards of the individual; but we do have, after all, reasonably effective techniques for accomplishing this. Moreover, this two-level approach is in fact demanded by the nature of the phenomenon.

Thus, several lines of research might be followed, and I mention these illustratively. We might study the behavioral consequences of individual perception of expectancies, under varying motivational conditions; the accuracy of such perception under levels of restriction of environmental cues, or as a function of individual "capacity," holding motivation constant; and, the effects of perceived conformity (or nonconformity) by various persons, serving as social stimulus objects, upon the behavior toward each of them by the perceiver.

In this regard, we have conducted one recent experiment, reported in the next chapter. On a problem-solving task, extended over numerous trials, we manipulated the time of nonconformity from group-established procedural norms by one member; his high-level of performance was held constant, however, for all treatments. Thus we find that his influence, as a status measure, is differently altered not only by the amount of nonconformity or its sheer extension in time, but reasonably enough by its *time placement*. Early evidences of nonconformity are more damaging to influence than the same degree of nonconformity displayed later; indeed, these later manifestations, if anything, are accepted as a basis for norm shifts—but, by then, understandably, the object person has already gained a predicted following from his previous record of performance and conformity.

If nothing else, this kind of study moves closer to the reality of life. Conformity behavior is elicited from most of us in a richer context than is provided by a situation where one either agrees or disagrees with a judgment made by four other people. Moreover, as a complexly determined output of interaction, manifest conformity by itself does not appear to be a very meaningful variable of personality.

17

Competence and conformity in the acceptance of influence

When one member influences others in his group it is often because he is competent in a focal group activity. A member may show such competence by individual actions that further the attainment of group goals (cf. Carter, 1954); more specific situational demands may variously favor the ascent of the expediter, advocate, or what Bales and Slater (1955) have termed the task specialist. An additional condition for the acceptance of influence involves the member's perceived adherence to the normative behaviors and attitudes of his group. His record of conformity to these expectancies serves to sustain eligibility of a sort.

As previously considered here, a person who exhibits both competence and conformity should eventually reach a threshold at which it becomes appropriate in the eyes of others for him to assert influence; and insofar as these assertions are accepted he emerges as a leader. To account for the "nonconformity" that leaders display as they innovate and alter group norms, certain shifts must occur in the expectancies applicable to an individual as he proceeds from gaining status to maintaining it. Such differentiations are a function of status, conceived in terms of "idio-

Adapted from the *Journal of Abnormal and Social Psychology*, 1960, 61, 365-369, with permission of the publisher, the American Psychological Association.

syncrasy credits." A person gains credits, i.e. rises in status, by showing competence and by conforming to the expectancies applicable to him at the time. Eventually his credits allow him to nonconform with greater impunity. Moreover, he is then subject to a new set of expectancies which direct the assertion of influence.

Problem

It is readily predictable that in task-oriented groups a member giving evidence of competence on the group task should gain in influence with time. If he simply nonconforms to the procedures agreed upon, the opposite effect should be observed. But the sequential relationship of nonconformity to competence is especially critical. With a relatively constant level of manifest competence, the influence of a person who nonconforms *early* in the course of group interaction should be more drastically curtailed than in the case of a person who nonconforms *later*. Indeed, a reversal of effect would be predicted in the latter instance. Once a member has accumulated credits, his nonconformity to general procedure should serve as a confirming or signalizing feature of his status, thereby enhancing his influence. Accordingly, it may be hypothesized that given equivalent degrees of task competence, a member should achieve greater acceptance of his influence when he has conformed in the past and is now nonconforming than he should when nonconformity precedes conformity.

Method

DESIGN

Twelve groups, each composed of four male subjects, were engaged in a task involving a sequence of 15 trials. A group choice was required for each trial from among the row alternatives in a 7×7 payoff matrix (see Figure 1). In every group, a fifth member was a confederate whose prearranged response was contrived to be correct on all but four trials, i.e. 2, 3, 6, and 12, thus reflecting con-

siderable competence on the task. All interactions among participants took place through a system of microphones and headsets
from partitioned booths. Subjects were assigned numbers from 1
to 5 for communicating with one another. The central manipulation was the confederate's nonconformity to procedures agreed
upon by each group in a pre-trial discussion. In terms of a division
of the 15 trials into three zones—early, middle, and late—of 5 trials
each, six treatments were applied: nonconformity throughout, nonconformity for the first two zones, for the first zone alone, for the
last two zones, for the last zone alone, and a control with no
nonconformity. In one set of treatments the confederate was designated number 5, and in the other number 4, to test possible position effects. Acceptance of the confederate's influence was measured by the number of trials by zone in which his recommended
response was accepted as the group's. This was supplemented by
post-interaction assessments.

	Green	Red	Blue	Yellow	Brown	Orange	Black
Able	−1	−12	+5	−1	−2	+15	−4
Baker	+10	−1	−2	−7	+4	−3	−1
Charlie	−5	+5	−3	+3	−11	−1	+12
Dog	+5	−7	+10	−2	−5	+1	−2
Easy	−4	−1	−1	+1	+13	−10	+2
Fox	−6	+15	−5	−1	−3	−1	+1
George	−1	−1	−2	+10	+4	−2	−8

Fig. 1. Matrix used in group task.

SUBJECTS
The 48 subjects were all juniors in the College of Engineering and
Science at the Carnegie Institute of Technology. All had volunteered from introductory psychology sections after being told only
that they would be taking part in a study of problem solving in
groups. Care was taken in composing the 12 groups so as to avoid
either placing acquaintances together or having membership
known in advance. Thus, no two subjects from the same class

section were used in the same group, and subjects reported at staggered times to different rooms. By the time a subject reached the laboratory room where the experiment was actually conducted, he had been kept apart from the others and was not aware of their identity. The subjects never saw one another during the entire procedure, nor were their names ever used among them.

INSTRUCTIONS AND SET

Once seated and assigned a number, every subject was given a sheet of instructions and the matrix used for the task. These instructions fell into two parts, both of which were reviewed aloud with each subject individually, and then with the entire group over the communication network. The first part cautioned the subjects always to identify themselves by number (e.g. "This is Station 3 . . .") before speaking and not to use names or other self-identifying references. The second part acquainted them with the procedures to be used, emphasized the aspect of competition against a "system," and established the basis for evident procedural norms. It read as follows:

1. You will be working with others on a problem involving a matrix of plus and minus values. Everyone has the same matrix before him. The goal is to amass as many plus units as possible, and to avoid minus units. Units are worth 1 cent each to the group; the group begins with a credit of 200 units. You cannot lose your own money, therefore. There will be fifteen trials in all.

2. In any one trial, the task involved is for the group to agree on just *one* row—identified by Able, Baker, Charlie, etc.—which seems to have strategic value. Once the group has determined a row, the experimenter will announce the column color which comes up on that trial. The intersecting cells indicate the payoff. Following this announcement, there will be thirty seconds of silence during which group members can think individually about the best strategy for the next trial, in terms of their notion about the system; note that there are several approximations to

the system, although the equation underlying it is quite complex. But work at it.

3. At the beginning of each trial the group members must report, one at a time, in some order, as to what they think would be the best row choice on the upcoming trial. Members may "pass" until the third time around, but must announce a choice then. Following this, groups will have three minutes on each trial to discuss choices and reach some agreement; this can be a simple majority, or unanimous decision; it is up to the group to decide. If a decision is not reached in three minutes, the group loses 5 units.

4. Before beginning the trials, the group will have five minutes to discuss these points: (a) The order of reporting; (b) How to determine the group choice for a given trial; (c) How to divide up the money at the end. These decisions are always subject to change, if the group has time and can agree. After the 15th trial, group members may have as much as five minutes to settle any outstanding decisions. Then headsets are to be removed, but group members remain seated for further instructions, and the individual payment of funds.

INSTRUMENTS AND PROCEDURE

The matrix was specially constructed for this study to present an ambiguous but plausible task in which alternatives were only marginally discrete from one another. The number of columns and rows was selected to enlarge the range of possibilities beyond the number of group members, while still retaining comprehensibility. The fact that the rows are unequal in algebraic sum appears to be less important as a feature in choice than the number and magnitude of positive and negative values in each; there is moreover the complicating feature of processing the outcome of the last trial in evaluating the choice for the next. All considered, the matrix was admirably suited to the requirements for ambiguity, challenge, conflict, immediate reinforcement, and ready manipulation by the experimenter.

The confederate, operating as either 4 or 5 in the groups, suggested a choice that differed trial by trial from those offered by other members; this was prearranged but subject to modification as required. Since subjects rather typically perceived alternatives differently, his behavior was not unusual, especially during the early trials. For the 11 trials in which the confederate's row choice was "correct," the color that "came up" was contrived to yield a high plus value without at the same time providing a similar value for intersection with another person's row choice. Had his recommendation been followed by the group on these trials, high payoffs would have accrued.

The device of a 5-minute pre-trial discussion had special utility for establishing common group expectancies, in the form of procedures, from which the confederate could deviate when called for in the design. Predictable decisions on these matters were reached unfailingly. But their importance lay in having a *public affirmation* of member intent. Thus, on order of reporting, it was quickly agreed to follow the order of the numbers assigned members. Each group, despite minor variants suggested, decided on simple majority rule. Regarding division of funds, equal sharing prevailed, sometimes with the proviso that the issue be taken up again at the end.

In the zones calling for nonconformity, the confederate violated these procedures by speaking out of prescribed turn, by questioning the utility of majority rule, and by unsupported—but not harsh—challenges to the recommendations made by others. He manifested such behaviors on an approximate frequency of at least one of these per trial with a mean of two per trial considered optimum. Thus, he would break in with his choice immediately after an earlier respondent had spoken and before the next in sequence could do so; when there were periods of silence during a trial he would observe aloud that maybe majority rule did not work so well; and he would show a lack of enthusiasm for the choice offered by various others on the matter of basis. Lest he lose credibility and become a caricature, in all instances he chose his moments with care and retained an evident spontaneity of expression.

Results and discussion

The task gave quite satisfactory signs of engrossing the subjects. There was much talk about the "system" and a good deal of delving into its basis, possibly intensified by the subjects' academic background; the returned matrices were littered with diagrams, notations, and calculations. Though quite meaningless in fact, the confederate's tentative accounts of his "reasoning" were evidently treated with seriousness, perhaps as much because of the contrived time constraint, which prevented probing, as of his jargon regarding "rotations" and "block shifts." In any case, the confederate at no time claimed to have the system completely in hand. He delayed his response from the sixth trial onward to suggest calculation of an optimum choice in the face of conflicting alternatives; and the four trials on which he was "wrong" were spaced to signify progressive improvement, but not total perfection.

Most pertinent, however, is the fact that there were no manifestations of suspicion concerning the confederate's authenticity. The others seemed to believe that he was one of them and that he was "cracking" the system; the post-interaction data were in full agreement.

Since all of the interactions were available on tape, it was possible to derive a number of indices of acceptance of influence. The most broadly revealing of these appeared to be the frequency of trials on which the confederate's recommended solution was followed.

In Table 1 this index is employed to discern the effects of three major variables. The analysis is arranged by zones (Z) of trials, and in terms of the confederate's nonconformity (NC) in the *current* zone and immediate *past* zone. For Zone I, the "past zone" refers to the discussion period. If he was to nonconform there, the confederate would question majority rule and suggest that the division

TABLE 1

Mean number of trials on which a group accepts confederate's recommended solution

Confederate's previous conformity	Zone I (Trials 1-5)		Zone II (Trials 6-10)		Zone III (Trials 11-15)	
	Noncon-forming [a]	Con-forming	Noncon-forming	Con-forming	Noncon-forming	Con-forming
With Procedural noncon-formity in imme-diate *past* zone	1.67 6 [b]	—	3.25 4	3.00 2	4.00 4	5.00 2
Without Procedural noncon-formity in imme-diate *past* zone	—	2.00 6	5.00 2	3.75 4	5.00 2	4.75 4

Analysis of variance

Source	SS	df	MS	F
Current Nonconformity	.20	1	.200	—
Zones	47.05	2	23.525	35.01 **
Past Nonconformity	3.36	1	3.360	5.00 *
Int: Current NC × Z	1.22	2	.610	—
Int: Current NC × Past NC	13.52	1	13.520	20.12 **
Int: Z × Past NC	.72	2	.360	—
Int: Current NC × Z × Past NC	4.11	2	2.055	3.06
Residual	16.12	24	.672	
Total	86.30	35		

Confederate showed procedural nonconformity on the trials in this zone.
Indicates number of groups upon which cell is based.
$p < .05$.
* $p < .001$.

of funds be left until the end rather than agree then on equal shares.

The means given in each cell of Table 1 indicate the number of trials, out of five per zone, on which the confederate's choice was also the group's. In a chi square test, the effect of position upon this measure was found to be nonsignificant, and is therefore omitted as a distinction in the analysis of variance.

The significant F secured from zones is in accord with prediction. It reveals the ongoing effect of task competence in increasing the acceptance of the confederate's choice, to be seen in the rising means across zones. While current nonconformity does not yield a significant effect, past nonconformity does. Viewing the table horizontally, one finds that the means for "without" *past* NC exceed the means for "with" *past* NC in all instances but one. Regarding the significant interaction of *current* and *past* NC, the combination "without-without" has a sequence (2.00, 3.75, 4.75) of persistently higher value than has "with-with" (1.67, 3.25, 4.00); this, too, is in line with prediction. Finally, the maximum value of 5.00 in Zone II for the combination "without" *past* NC but "with" *current* NC confirms the key prediction from the model, at least within the context of the relative magnitudes there; the same value is also seen in Zone III for the identical combination still another reading of 5.00 holds there, however, for the inverse combination, but in a tight range of values quite beyond separation of effects for interpretation.

Considerable consistency was found too in the post-interaction data. On the item "overall contribution to the group activity," 44 of the 48 subjects ranked the confederate first; on the item "influence over the group's decisions," 45 of the 48 ranked him first. Two things bear emphasis in this regard: subjects had to individually write in the numbers of group members next to rank, hence demanding recall; and their polarity of response cut across all six treatments, despite significant differences among these in the actual *acceptance of influence*. That the confederate therefore made an impact is clear; but that it had selective consequences depending upon the timing of his nonconformity is equally clear.

In detail, then, the findings are in keeping with the predictions made. The operational variable for measuring acceptance of influence was confined to the task itself, but nontask elements are touched as well. In that respect, the findings corroborate the subtle development of differential impressions as a function of even limited interpersonal behavior.

Some unquantified but clearly suggestive data are worth mentioning in this regard. Where, for example, the confederate began nonconforming *after* the first zone, his behavior was accepted with minimal challenge; by the third zone, his suggestion that majority rule was faulty yielded a rubber stamping of his choice. Again, if he had already accrued credit, his pattern of interrupting people out of turn not only went unhindered but was taken up by some others. Quite different effects were elicited if the confederate exhibited nonconformity from *the outset*, notably such comments of censure as "That's not the way we agreed to do it, five."

The findings are especially indicative of the stochastic element of social interaction and its consequence for changing perception. Especially interesting is the fact that these effects are produced even in a relatively brief span of time.

Summary

A study was conducted to test the relationship between competence on a group task and conformity or nonconformity to procedural norms in determining a person's ability to influence other group members. Data were gathered from 12 groups engaged in a problem solving task under controlled conditions. Each was made up of five members one of whom was a confederate who evidenced a high degree of competence during the 15 trials. His nonconformity to the procedural norms agreed upon by the group was introduced at various times, early, middle, or late, in the sequence of trials. Influence was measured by the number of trials (per segment of the entire sequence) in which the confederate's recommended solution was accepted as the group's choice. As a broad effect, it was found that a significant increase in his influence occurred as the trials progressed, presumably as a function of the successive evidences of competence. Past conformity by the confederate was also found to be positively and significantly related to the acceptance of his influence; finally, there was a statistically significant interaction between past and current nonconformity reflected in high influence in the groups in which the confederate had conformed earlier in the sequence of trials but was presently nonconforming. These results were consistent with predictions made from the "idiosyncrasy credit" model of conformity and status.

18

Some effects of perceived status on responses to innovative behavior

What one member of a group may do with impunity another may not do. This observation fits many circumstances of social inter- action and serves as a central element in the "idiosyncrasy credit" model of perceived status and conformity. In terms of the model, evidences that a person is competent in some focal group activity, and that he has conformed to applicable group expectancies, result in his accumulating credits that he may draw on later for inno- vative behaviors directed at exercising influence. A study of these relationships is presented in the preceding chapter.

Another illustration of the operational aspects of perceived status is provided by an experiment reported in Pepitone (1958, p. 266), where subjects were presented with a script of a technical discussion and were given varying prior sets as to the level of expert qualification of one of the two participants; the greater the alleged expertness of that person, the more favorable were the subjects' interpretations of his negative acts as well as of his positive ones.

Adapted from the *Journal of Abnormal and Social Psychology*, 1961, 63, 247- 250, with permission of the publisher, the American Psychological Association.

Problem

The present experiment follows a simple, two-step approach in further studying differences in response to behavior as a function of the perceived status of the behaving person. First, it may be predicted that attributing higher degrees of competence to a person should result in correspondingly greater willingness to accept that person's authority. Further, this effect should be enhanced for each degree of ascribed competence the longer the person is known to have belonged to the group; all things constant, the equally competent newcomer to the group should have less authority than his counterpart who has been there longer. Second, the status thus accorded the person described should be inversely related to disapproval of his deviancy, i.e. the higher the status, the less the disapproval. This relation should hold especially in the case of innovative deviancy. In short, the intent is to induce levels of perceived status so as to discern their effect upon responses to given behaviors. To produce status experimentally, the first step of this approach makes use of the direct "trait description" technique employed by Asch (1946), in his study of impressions of personality, and more recently by Bruner, Shapiro, and Tagiuri (1958).

Method

SUBJECTS, SETTING, AND SET

One hundred and fifty-one undergraduate students enrolled in lower-level psychology courses at Washington University were utilized as subjects. Sixty-four were males, and 87 females. All fell within the age range of 18-23, with a mean about 20. The entire procedure was conducted in class sections, after an introductory statement by the investigator that this was a study of attitudes in groups and that responses would be anonymous. Forms with precise instructions were then distributed.

PROCEDURE

The first form instructed subjects to think of a group to which they belonged, at the time or before, and to imagine in it a person of their own sex who was described by a succinct set of terms which followed. Then the form asked: "Knowing this information, how willing would you be to have this person in a position of authority in the group?" Responses were made on a seven-point scale labeled "definitely not" at one end, "very willing" at the other, and "neutral" in the middle.

Each subject received a single description made up of four terms, of which two were varied, and two held constant, throughout. Competence in the group's activity, arrayed at four degrees, was paired with one of two levels of time in group to provide eight descriptions of the stimulus person within a 2 × 4 design: thus either "been in group for some while" or "new to group" appeared in combination with "extremely capable performer in group's activity," or "capable performer in group's activity," or "average performer in group's activity," or "poor performer in group's activity." The constant terms, "interested" and "generally liked," were used to control for two other determinants of status postulated in the model, "motivation to belong" and "beta value." Examples of the resulting descriptions are given by the two extremes below:

Extremely capable performer in group's activity.
Been in group for some while. Interested.
Generally liked.

Poor performer in group's activity.
New to group. Interested.
Generally liked.

Having made their ratings, subjects were then given a second form instructing them to think again of the *same group* with the person of their own sex once again described *exactly as before*. Eight behaviors were presented to afford a range of stimuli for responses linked to status. The first of these—"suggests changes from group plans"—was of special significance in terms of the influence aspect of status. The others, in order, were: "speaks freely about other group members," "questions the views of other group members," "performs tasks independently," "interrupts to express comments at group meeting," "discusses group concerns with outsiders," "makes own decisions on attending group functions," and "casual in relations with other group members." All were selected as illustrative of intragroup behaviors that might be variously interpreted and were based on responses to an open-ended question from a similar but independent group of subjects. In this second step, subjects indicated for each of these eight behaviors whether their evaluation of the stimulus person would go up or go down, and by what percentage weight, if he displayed it.

Scores for accorded status were readily derived from the rating responses made to the question concerning willingness to have the stimulus person in a position of authority. These were scaled from 7 for "very willing" to 1 for "definitely not" with 4 assigned to "neutral." The distribution of these scores was inclined toward the upper values with a mean of 4.5, a median and mode of 5, and a standard deviation of 1.6.

Results and discussion

Table 1 presents the means for the accorded status score by experimental treatments, the N's for which varied from 17 to 22. In both columns the values proceed steadily upward in line with the rising degrees of competence ascribed to the stimulus person. At each degree, those said to be in the group longer receive a higher mean score on this status measure. These relationships are made graphic in Figure 1. An analysis of variance completed for these data yielded significant F values for both major variables, but no for sex difference or any of the interaction terms.

Because of marked intersubject variability in the "percentage weight" response, the measure of disapproval employed for th

TABLE 1

Means for accorded status by experimental treatments

Treatment	In group for some while	New to group
Extremely capable performer	6.25	5.84
Capable performer	6.11	5.50
Average performer	5.06	4.50
Poor performer	2.95	2.53

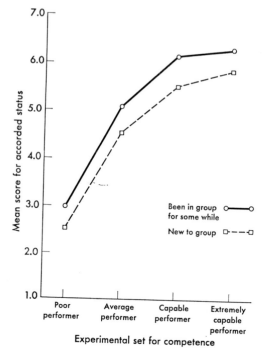

Fig. 1. Scores for accorded status by two levels of time in group and set for competence.

second part of the experiment was the *percentage of subjects responding "down"* for each behavior, by the level of status previously accorded the stimulus person. These data were viewed in two ways. The difference in disapproval for each behavior, across status, was tested for significance by chi square, revealing only "suggests changes" to have a value significant beyond the .05 level. Second, levels of accorded status were correlated (rho) with ranks for magnitude of disapproval. A high negative coefficient signifies a *decrease* in disapproval as status *increases*, in keeping with prediction. This was in fact the case for two behaviors with significant coefficients: the key innovative behavior "suggests changes from group plans" ($-.96$), and "discusses group concerns with outsiders" ($-.74$). The pattern of rho values for the other behaviors was not uniformly negative. Of the three with positive signs, only one approximated significance, that being "interrupts to express comments at group meeting" ($+.68$).

In Figure 2 curves are plotted for the two behaviors with significant values for rho and for the one with a value nearly so. Most marked is the curve for "suggests changes," the behavior most closely tied to the assertion of influence. Disapproval of this behavior drops off quite systematically with rising accorded status. A similar though less sharp effect is seen for "discusses with outsiders," a behavior connected with the spokesman or advocate function; while not approved at any level, at the two lowest reaches of accorded status this is disapproved by all respondents.

A contrasting effect is seen in the positive curve for "interrupts," suggesting that this behavior is less likely to alter the evaluation of a person of lower status than one of higher status. This interpretation fits the proposition that shifts in expectancies are associated with increased status. In this instance, and as part of a probable democratic image of leadership, it becomes more crucial in conserving credits for the high status member than for the low status member not to interrupt others in the group.

The findings of this experiment provide evidence of directly discernible inputs to status, from competence and time in group.

resulting in consistent response tendencies. These effects are the more noteworthy for having been produced irrespective of the nature of the group—a choice left to each subject individually—and with only minimal stimulus material.

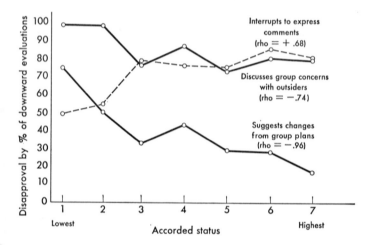

Fig. 2. Percentage of respondents giving downward evaluation of stimulus person for displaying indicated behaviors, by status accorded the stimulus person.

Summary

An experiment was conducted to test postulates from the "idiosyncrasy credit" model of status. A brief description of a person they were to imagine in any group to which they belonged was presented to 151 subjects of both sexes. Competence and length of time in the group were the major attributes manipulated. These were paired in eight descriptions, only one of which was given to each subject as a treatment. Responses were then made on a seven-point scale to signify willingness to have that person in a position of authority in the group, and this served as an index of accorded status. A rising mean score for accorded status was found for the increasing degrees of competence, and the mean for "new to group" was uniformly lower than that for "in group for some while" at each degree. The effects of these two major variables was significant, while sex difference was not. Subjects also provided an evaluation of the same person in terms of eight possible ways he might behave in the group. According to prediction, two behaviors reflecting innovative action were found to be disapproved significantly less the higher the status attributed to the innovator.

19

Conformity, independence, and anticonformity as determiners of perceived influence and attraction

WITH RICHARD H. WILLIS

When two persons work together on a common task several things
become relevant in their relationship. Among these are competence
in the task itself, and responsiveness to one another's judgment.
The latter may consist of the responses from one person showing
essentially (a) agreement or conformity, (b) rejection or "anticonformity," or (c) independence, relative to judgments made by
the other. In this paper we report an experiment which looked at
several consequences arising from the arrangement of various combinations of these modes of response and relative competence for
a pair of co-workers.

A recent study by the writers has shown how responses of conformity, independence, and anticonformity may be produced by
the controlled manipulation in dyads of certain independent vari-

Presented before the 1964 Eastern Psychological Association Convention at
Philadelphia.

213

ables, among them competence of the co-worker (Willis & Hollander, 1964). The basis for that study was the Willis response model (1963, 1964) which embodies two dimensions rather than the more usual single dimension (e.g. Asch, 1956; Jahoda, 1959) to represent conformity-nonconformity; these two dimensions generate the three modes of response indicated above. The Willis and Hollander study demonstrated that the different outcomes seen as independence or anticonformity behavior arise from different sources.

Since these two varieties of nonconforming behavior may be aroused and distinguished from one another as *dependent* variables, it seems reasonable to expect that as *independent* variables each will produce discriminable effects on co-workers. As reported here in Chapters 17 and 18, it has been shown experimentally that nonconformity is reacted to variously as a function of the perceived status of the actor, quite apart from the earlier and broader Schachter finding (1951). This feature of status is treated in Chapter 15 in the idiosyncrasy credit model (Hollander, 1958), one proposition of which is that nonconforming behavior is perceived differentially by the group, depending upon the amount of credit the individual has built up through previous conformity and demonstrated competence. The more credit the individual has at his disposal, the more positively will his "nonconformity" be evaluated by the rest of the group. However, credit would be expected to be put to use for the facilitation of independence behavior, not usually for an actual negation of normative prescriptions, as in anticonformity. Thus, Willis's model of social response poses the question of whether independence can be shown to be more positively valued than anticonformity when a member has demonstrated competence and so has accrued credits.

Problem

In the experiment reported here, the three modes of response from the Willis model are employed as independent variables and, at the same time, apparent task competence is also manipulated so as to make the subject believe that he himself, or the co-worker, or both are competent.

The major dependent variables are (1) the perceived influence of the co-worker following successive trials, and also (2) the willingness on the part of the subject to work with that co-worker again, as a measure of interpersonal attraction. It is predicted that the value of both of these variables will depend upon the interaction of the co-worker's competence and his mode of response. Specifically, both perceived influence and interpersonal attraction are expected to be maximal under conditions of co-worker competence and independence of judgment. Furthermore, subjects are predicted to react differently to independence and anticonformity behavior on the part of co-workers.

Procedure

SUBJECTS

Fifty-four male undergraduate students, enrolled in the introductory psychology course at the State University of New York at Buffalo, participated as subjects. Preponderantly freshmen and sophomores, they ranged in age from 17 to 23 with the mode falling at 18.

DESIGN

A two-factor design was employed with three levels for each factor. The three modes of social response exhibited by the co-worker—conformity, independence, and anticonformity—were manipulated as the levels of one factor. Orthogonal to these, three competence sets were induced such that the subject believed that he was competent, or that his co-worker was competent, or, in the third case, that both he and his co-worker were competent.[1] Six subjects were randomly assigned to each of the nine experimental conditions thus created.

TASK AND STIMULUS MATERIALS

Subjects were asked to judge the prize-winning quality of each of ten pictures presented one at a time as experimental trials. The set of pictures was obtained from a prominent photography magazine and all were of prize-winning quality. None of the pictures had people as central or primary content. Each picture was approximately 5 × 7 inches and was mounted on an 8 × 10 inch mat. On first viewing each picture, every subject first indicated on a scale from one to five how much he *personally liked* each picture. Then he, and ostensibly his co-worker, judged whether or not each picture was of prize-winning quality. These were simple binary, yes or no, judgments. Nothing was said to indicate how many "prize-winners" were in the set so that no constraint was imposed on the number of affirmative judgments a subject believed he could make.

EXPERIMENTAL SETTING AND INSTRUCTIONS

Although each subject was given to understand that he was paired with a co-worker, the arrangement allowed a controlled interaction with a "co-worker" whose responses were simulated by the passage to the subject of appropriate notes. Subjects were led into the laboratory individually and placed in cubicles without seeing or having any contact with other subjects present. Every subject believed that he was B in a pair A and B. Subjects were run in groups of at least two, and sometimes as many as four.

Once in the cubicle, the subject was provided with an instruction sheet indicating that he and a co-worker were to arrive at a com-

[1] Twenty-two additional subjects were run as controls. These control conditions combined the three modes of co-worker response with two supplementary competence treatments, viz. neither subject nor co-worker competent, and no indication whatever of competence. Either three or four subjects were run in each of these six conditions. Results show only that the manipulations to induce a competence set for the main experimental treatments were successful.

mon judgment about the prize-winning quality of each of the pictures which were stacked face down before him. The instructions indicated that there were to be no oral communications and that each message concerning individual judgments of the pictures would be passed through a slot to the experimenter who would record it and pass it on to the co-worker.

Person A (always the co-worker) was presumed to make a first judgment at the same time that the actual subject (always **B**) made his one and only judgment of each picture. These first judgments were to be exchanged, and then A would make another judgment. The instructions which subjects read said: "*If you are A you will make the last judgment for the pair. This judgment will be taken as the indication of how successful the pair is in judging the photographs.*" Therefore, each subject, as B, knew that he would make just *one* judgment for each picture, and that it *might or might not have an effect upon A's second judgment* which would serve as the indication of their common choice.

TREATMENTS

In all experimental and control treatments, then, the procedure was such that each subject believed that he was B and that the co-worker was A. From the subject's point of view, he saw a picture, he indicated his personal liking for it on a five-point scale, and finally he placed on a slip of paper a *plus* or a *minus* as his judgment of whether or not it was a prize winner, with no limit whatever on the use of plusses among the ten judgments. So far as he was informed, that judgment would then be turned over to A after he passed it through the slot. Thereafter, as if by exchange, the subject received A's *first* judgment, followed within a minute by A's *second* judgment. On the sheet before him each subject kept a record of all of his own responses and those of his co-worker.

A set for competence was introduced by informing subjects that, for the first three pictures, A and B would both see the second judgment (made by A) after it had been marked by the experimenter to indicate whether it was right or wrong. Exercising this device, it was possible to make it appear that either the subject alone, the co-worker alone, or both were correct in judging all three of these first pictures.[2] Following the introduction of this set, one and *only one* mode of response, either conformity, independence, or anticonformity, was used consistently for each of the last seven pictures, in the fashion shown in Table 1.

TABLE 1

Program of co-worker judgments for three response patterns in each of seven pictures by subject's positive or negative judgment

	Subject's judgment			
	Positive (+)		Negative (−)	
Mode of co-worker response	Co-worker's first judgment	Co-worker's second judgment	Co-worker's first judgment	Co-worker's second judgment
Conformity	−	+	+	−
Independence	−	−	+	+
	(4 pictures)		(4 pictures)	
	+	+	−	−
	(3 pictures)		(3 pictures)	
Anticonformity	+	−	−	+

As will be noted in Table 1, *conformity* consists of a shift between the co-worker's first and second judgments reflecting an apparent movement toward the judgment made by the subject. For *independence*, the co-worker's first and second judgments in

[2] A limitation presented was that under the condition where "both" are competent, the conformity response must imply a conflict insofar as the first response of A and B must be different for A to then appear to be agreeing with B. Thus, "both" were "right"—but on A's second judgment, not his first—for the first three pictures. Similarly, "both" involves a requirement for similar first choices in the "independence" condition, so that an isomorphism of judgment on the first three pictures had to occur there. No systematic effects were traceable to these minor variants.

every instance are the same, indicating an evident indifference to the subject's judgments he is presumed to have seen. Since independence is not characterized by negativism, but rather by a consistent disregard of the partner's view, this treatment consisted of a different judgment than the subject's on four pictures and the same judgment on three pictures (numbers 4, 6, and 9), though not affected by the subject. In *anticonformity*, the co-worker makes the same judgment of the first picture, but moves to the reverse judgment following the apparent discovery that he and the subject made similar first judgments. Here, then, the co-worker takes full account of the judgments of the subject, but in the reverse fashion constituting pure anticonformity behavior.

DEPENDENT VARIABLES

Measures of the major dependent variables were obtained from questionnaires administered to subjects in the post-interaction phase, immediately following the judgment of all pictures. Response sheets were taken from subjects and each then responded on another sheet to two key items in particular. The first of these, referred to here as "perceived influence," asked the subject to circle a number from one to five on a scale from lowest to highest influence indicating "How influenced do you believe you were by your co-worker?" For the second key item, referred to here as "interpersonal attraction," the subject indicated on another five-point scale his reaction to "How much would you be satisfied to do a similar task again with the *same* co-worker?"

A measure of the third dependent variable, referred to here as a "liking for pictures," was obtained during the judgmental period. It will be recalled that each subject indicated, prior to each plus-minus judgment, his personal liking for that picture. It should be noted that these personal evaluations were privately recorded and never transmitted to the co-worker.

Results and discussion

An immediate question concerns the differential production of effects. More specifically, do the two varieties of nonconformity—independence and anticonformity—yield discriminably different reactions toward co-workers? And if so, do these differential reactions depend in an interactive manner upon the various competence treatments? The answers obtained to these questions, as revealed in Tables 2 and 3, are both affirmative.

TABLE 2

Means for perceived influence of co-worker by major treatments

Mode of co-worker behavior	Competence			Row mean
	Self	Co-worker	Both	
Conformity	1.33	1.83	1.00	1.39
Independence	1.50	2.17	2.00	1.89
Anticonformity	1.00	1.33	1.17	1.17
Column mean	1.28	1.78	1.39	1.48

TABLE 3

Means for work with co-worker again by major treatments

Mode of co-worker behavior	Competence			Row mean
	Self	Co-worker	Both	
Conformity	2.17	2.33	3.33	2.61
Independence	1.67	3.17	3.17	2.67
Anticonformity	2.50	2.83	3.00	2.78
Column mean	2.11	2.78	3.17	2.68

Before proceeding to a detailed discussion of results, it is worthwhile noting that the correlation between the two post-interaction measures, as represented in these tables, was .04, or essentially zero. This indicates a quite different basis for these two kinds of evaluations of co-workers.

Means for the measure of perceived influence are given in Table 2 for each of the experimental treatments. The overall mean was 1.48 and individual cell means (N = 6 for each) varied from a high of 2.17, occurring in the case of competent and independent co-workers, to a low of 1.00 appearing in two of the cells. Analysis of variance yielded an F ratio significant at the .05 level for the effect of mode of co-worker response, but nonsignificant values of F for the competence main effect and for the interaction effect. Independence had the highest row mean, while anticonformity had the lowest, and this difference is significant at the .05 level.

Comparing cells within Table 2, the Duncan multiple range test (Duncan, 1955; Edwards, 1960, pp. 136-140) indicated a significant difference at the .05 level for two intercell differences, those for the highest mean (co-worker competent and independent) against the two lowest means (subject competent and co-worker anticonforming, and both competent and co-worker conforming).

In interpreting these findings, it is essential to bear in mind the fact that the subject made only *one* judgment for *each* picture, and that—unlike classic studies of convergence—there was no possibility, in any *one* trial viewed alone, for the subject actually to be influenced by his co-worker's judgments. On that basis, then, all treatments would have yielded means of 1.00, i.e. lowest perceived influence, unless they reacted to whatever pattern of response the co-worker evidenced as a source of inter-trial influence. The fact that some means were substantially and significantly above this minimum value, despite these constraining conditions, indicates a differential enhancement of perceived influence from treatment to treatment, with the greatest effect evident in the central cell of Table 2.

The data for the other key post-interaction question, concerning interpersonal attraction for co-worker, are summarized in Table 3. Again, responses were on a five-point scale, ranging from lowest to highest attraction or acceptance of co-worker. Analysis of variance yielded an F ratio for the main effect due to competence significant just at the borderline of the .05 level. Neither the main effect due to mode of co-worker behavior nor the interaction effect was significant. Though no intercell differences quite reached significance at the .05 level, it is worth noting that the cell predicted to contain the highest mean (co-worker competent and independent), does in fact display one of the highest means in the table. Moreover, with respect to the significant major effect, it is evident that maximum attraction for co-worker occurs under the condition in which both are competent, while only the subject competent condition yields the lowest value. It is also worth calling attention to the fact that, overall, the conforming co-worker was *not* significantly preferred over the other two and indeed the anticonforming one had the high mean, as seen in Table 3.

Since the essential element of this experiment was to discern a variety of the effects produced by competence in combination with co-worker responses of the conforming, independence or anticonforming variety, personal liking for pictures was viewed as a way of probing the psychological effects on subjects of various treatments in time. In Table 4 the means for personal liking for the last seven pictures, following the competence inductions, are given for all major treatments. The data for this analysis have been transformed to hold variations in the mean likability of these seven

TABLE 4

Average discrepancy of liking for last seven pictures calculated from the mean liking of each picture by major treatments *

Mode of co-worker behavior	Competence			Row mean
	Self	Co-worker	Both	
Conformity	7.7	5.3	10.8	7.9
Independence	11.6	14.0	7.6	11.0
Anticonformity	9.7	8.8	13.3	10.6
Column mean	9.7	9.4	10.6	9.9

* Mean liking per picture set at 10 and deviations from mean multiplied by 10 for this analysis.

pictures approximately constant since that is not a relevant concern, and a prior analysis of variance had yielded a significant major effect for pictures. Quite simply, the grand mean of likability for each picture was converted to 10, and then cell variations were represented by 1 for each tenth of a point deviation above or below the grand mean for the picture. Each cell therefore was based upon these seven deviation scores, one for each of the seven pictures, and the means given reflect a composite outcome across those pictures. For these data, an analysis of variance yielded an F significant at the .01 level for the interaction of competence and mode of response, confirming the combinatorial effects predicted. Duncan range tests indicated a significant difference at the .05 level between the cell means for various combinations including independence with co-worker competent taken against both conformity and anticonformity with the co-worker competent.

It bears note that in Table 4 independence clearly yields the deviant patterning, with a relatively low mean for the both competent condition and relatively high means for the two remaining competence conditions. Both conformity and anticonformity display the reverse patterning, thereby exhibiting also a high degree of similarity to one another. Relevant to these findings is the consideration that the two-dimensional model of social response (Willis, 1962, 1963) specifies that conformity and anticonformity are *both* varieties of dependence behavior and thus differ in common from independence behavior, in this respect.

In assessing the findings of this investigation, it might be emphasized that the predictions confirmed are not of an entirely obvious kind. For example, one hypothesis which readily suggests itself predicts that subjects will feel themselves to be most influenced by co-workers in that condition in which the co-workers appeared to be most influenced by subjects, i.e. the conformity treatment. Yet in Table 2 the conformity treatment yields lower mean perceived influence than the independence treatment, for all three combinations of competence. Note also that the highest cell mean occurs when the co-worker is both competent and independent, as predicted, and that for this condition the number of agreements on the second judgment is merely three out of the ten possible. Thus, agreement has various meanings or value depending upon the context of who is competent and the co-worker's mode of response.

In various ways, then, it seems clear that conformity, independence, and anticonformity behavior elicit different effects in combination with competence. Therefore, it seems necessary not only to distinguish between conformity and nonconformity, but also to distinguish the independent variety of nonconformity from the anticonformity variety.

Summary

An experiment was conducted in which subjects worked with co-workers who characteristically either conformed to the subjects' judgments in the task, anticonformed to their judgments, or behaved independently, i.e. were evidently unaffected by the subjects' judgments. The effect of these three modes of co-worker behavior was studied in combination with each of three competence conditions in which the subject believed: 1) that he alone was competent on the task; 2) that the co-worker alone was competent; or 3) that both were competent. As predicted, highest perceived co-worker influence occurred under the condition where the co-worker behaved independently and was perceived as competent. Other differentiating effects were found, among them in the subjects' willingness to work with the co-worker again.

20

Leader effectiveness and
influence process

In this chapter we propose to do three things: first, elaborate the concept of idiosyncrasy credit to account further for certain of the mechanisms postulated in Chapter 15; second, derive some particular statements concerning "leader effectiveness"; and, third, explore several implications concerning influence as a general process.

Inescapably, the selecting and training of people for positions of leadership, especially within organizational settings, demand a sense of what makes leaders effective. Therefore, while there may not be "universal traits" of leadership, it is possible to speak of requisites for effective leadership. Our intent here is to consider what some of the most salient of these appear to be, recognizing that any one individual's leadership "style" may be uniquely effective for him. From this we shall go on to the more general issue of implications regarding influence process.

Clearly, various meanings can be offered for "leader effectiveness." In our view, it is best considered to be an influence process wherein the leader is able to muster willing group support, to achieve certain clearly specified group goals, with best advantage to the individuals comprising the group. Moreover, we shall not be distinguishing between emergent and imposed leadership despite our recognition that an important distinction between the two can be made. While the goals may be different, and the source of influence quite clearly is different, the operation of a group in terms of its movement toward a goal rests on characteristics which go beyond these distinctions alone. Our considerations here, therefore, have application to the organizationally imposed leader as well as to the one who emerges by group consent.

Influence potential and influence acceptance

In these last chapters, particularly Chapter 15, we have covered issues which bear on considerations of leadership functioning in terms of "idiosyncrasy credit." Two aspects of leadership in particular have been given attention. These are factors which in the first place determine a differentiation of status allowing for potential influence, and second, factors which interrelate to yield acceptance of that influence. Essentially, this represents the distinction between *attaining* versus *maintaining* leadership. The effectiveness of leadership refers to the latter process.

One central aspect of the concept of "emergent leadership" is the provision it makes for talking about group structure in terms of the development of status among group members. In this conception, potential influence may be increased or diminished depending upon the effects of ongoing interactions on persons as perceivers. The essential point here is that people retain a history of what has transpired in the past, even though that process need not be confining as a determiner of behavior since new experience is continuously having its effects.

Factors determining leader effectiveness

Among those factors we have thus far noted which shape the leader's effectiveness are his competence, his fulfillment of certain group expectancies for structure and action, his perceived motivation, and his adaptability to changing requirements of the situation. Before giving separate attention to each of these elements, it should be said that they are all relative rather than absolute in character. We are not reinstating certain trait conceptions of leadership but rather are pointing to qualities which have relevance to the attainment of group goals and which are defined within the context of the group's operation at a given time. As an example, we have said that status permits a degree of latitude for behavior in terms of common expectancies in a group. We have also said that there are certain restrictions imposed upon the high status person in terms of what may be thought of as particularized expectancies, that is, role behaviors. In short, the group defines which particulars have significance in terms of its context of operation.

PARTICULARIZED EXPECTANCIES

Our contention has been that role behaviors of leadership tend to be more highly prescribed. Why should this be so? Two reasons seem to apply here: as a first consideration, high status carries with it the assumption of greater initiative for action, as Thibaut and Riecken (1955) have demonstrated. The leader, as an exemplification of a high status person, is assumed to be more responsible for the actions that he displays. Equally important as a second consideration is that high status makes more stringent demands for certain roles because these carry responsibilities which are greater and more likely to affect important outcomes for the members of the group. As a person's status increases, he tends to occupy more and more important roles. Consequently, his fulfillment of the leadership function becomes more crucial to the group's achievement of its goal. Another way of viewing this is in terms of a simple figure-ground phenomenon. Actions which call attention to a person may lead him to a position of influence because of favorable outcomes. Then, since his activity now becomes more crucial to the group's attainment of goals, his visibility is even further increased.

Conformity depends upon the perception held of the actor, and what therefore may be perceived as nonconforming for one member of the group may not be perceived as nonconforming for another. The implication of this having specific regard to the effective functioning of leadership is this: the person who breaches a common expectancy of a group and in the process succeeds in helping the group to achieve its goal will be judged differently from the one who fails to do so in deviating. Thus, the outcome of any given act of nonconformity in terms of the group's function is an obvious point of reference for judging the actor. Though the nonconforming behavior of a higher status group member may be perceived more readily, it is likely to be interpreted in terms of certain positive outcomes, given the development of a history of past deviations which have proven to be fruitful innovations. There appears to be a kind of cognitive balancing induced where status is high and an individual has credit at his disposal; in general, his action is more likely to be perceived in the nature of providing good outcomes to the group rather than bad outcomes. This point of view has been further elaborated by Pauline Pepinsky in her concept of "productive nonconformity" (1961).

Furthermore, as March has pointed out (1954), norms themselves may actually have varying forms determining how "goodness" will be defined, i.e. the unattainable ideal, the attainable ideal, and the preferred value. Applying this analysis to the group expectancies we have been discussing, it is clear that there are some behaviors which could never completely fulfill the group's ideal, while others will readily be seen as falling in a range of distinctly preferred value.

MOTIVATIONAL ORIENTATIONS

Associated with nonconforming acts is the construction the group may put on the underlying motive for the action. As Heider (1958) indicates, the difference between object perception and person perception lies in the observation that in the latter case a motive will be imputed to explain the behavior exhibited. The fact that more favorable motivations are imputed to persons of higher status has been experimentally demonstrated in a number of studies, including one cited by Pepitone (1958) and noted earlier. Also, Thibaut and Riecken have found that the high status person who conforms is seen to do so for internally determined causes while the low status person is seen to conform for externally determined causes, that is, pressures from others. This means that the motivation seen to underlie the action varies as a function of the actor's perceived status and that the high status person is believed to command greater initiative to do as he wishes.

Still another important motive which may be perceived by others is the person's motivation to belong. And what most seems to matter about this is the sense the action gives of a self-aggrandizing orientation or group-sustaining orientation. While these divergences are not complete, they may not be readily perceived as compatible with one another. What appears to be especially important is that the leader's motivation be seen as high and sincere where group concerns are at stake.

All of these processes are subject to the enveloping effects of the environment, which can redefine the normative aspects of the social situation. As a consequence, it may not be enough merely to say that an act is normatively perceived as a "good" act, unless we add "relative to the then prevailing circumstances."

Attributive and behavioral qualities

A further consideration regarding norms is that they may have either attributive or behavioral quality. An example of an attributive quality would be represented in the expectancy that group members be white men, or at least that they be men. In such a case, the individual must bring an attribute to the situation quite apart from his actions. And that individual's actions may be misjudged because of an absence of the "proper" attributes, by not being white or male, as in the instance given.

Actual behaviors, on the other hand, represent an observable sequence of activity open to evaluation in terms of some desired goal. Behavioral qualities tend to take precedence as a member of the group attains higher levels of status, once having shown certain of the attributes which are considered to be requisite to a position of leadership. While credits may be awarded initially in terms of valued attributes, behaviors which are seen to fit certain of the expectancies of the group later serve as the major source. Given "proper" attributes, and then behaviors meshing with the expectancies of the group, there should be a rise in status with time. But, as previously noted, in the absence of some degree of appropriate action, credits may be "lost" through disuse because the signalizing behavioral features of leadership are not fulfilled.

COMPETENCE

An important attribute of the leader is his competence in some task which is of importance to the group's achievement of its goal, a matter we have particularly stressed in the foregoing chapters. While competence has been misinterpreted at times to mean some necessary ability on a task, in actuality there are many group situations in which the function may not be so much a task which literally produces a product as a set of characteristics which are demanded if the group is to operate smoothly in terms of its desires. In a highly sociable setting, for example, it may be that having a good sense of humor and facilitating the social interaction of members becomes important in terms of this matter of competence. Therefore we should understand the individual's functional value for the group as encompassing a wide variety of situationally determined demands for varying kinds of attributes. Competence, it is well to emphasize, is also time-bound in that what may be important to securing a goal at one juncture may no longer be important as the goal is achieved. Accordingly, re-definitions of competence may periodically occur. This may mean that as the group moves to a new set of task requirements the former leadership becomes inadequate for reasons of its incapability to meet these new demands. The requirement for perceptiveness in seeing these new demands is of course associated with this aspect of leadership maintenance.

IDENTIFICATION

In keeping with previous points, the leader must be seen by potential followers as having an identification with the group, in the sense of a clear involvement with the group's activity. Cartwright, in summarizing the implications of work on "group dynamics," has spoken of agents of change (1951). He indicates that a key characteristic of persons who are successful in this function is that they be seen to share an identification with the group in its circumstance. Apart from attributes as such, it is therefore important that the leader, by his behavior, manifest a loyalty to the needs and aspirations of group members. These things must matter to him in ways that are accessible to view because such evidences of good faith and sincere interest serve to elicit greater acceptance of influence for reasons spelled out later.

Behavioral processes

In addition to the two attributes of competence and identification with the group, there are several behavioral processes which seem to be important in determining the effectiveness of leadership. These may be considered under three general headings: first, providing the group with structure and goal-setting, as Hemphill has suggested (1958); second, maintaining a flexibility and adaptability in handling changing requirements as new situations develop; and, third, establishing productive social relationships which arise from a predictability of behavior on the leader's part which manifests itself in emotional stability, dependability, and fairness in distributing rewards. Recognizing that these behaviors are always achieved and defined within the group's structure, and may

therefore vary in specific content as well as in the goals actually
sought, let us consider what some of the implications of these
would be.

COMMUNICATION

For the leader to establish structure, it is essential that he foster
communication within the group by providing mechanisms for
participation and for the need that members be informed in advance of decisions or actions that will affect them. Adaptability to
new situations also requires communication within the group.
Thus, several ends of effective leadership are served by facilitating
an exchange of information.

The fact that groups continually face new situations which require innovation means that the effective leader, while he may be
an "idea man" in his own right, recognizes the potential merit in
the good ideas of others. This is, of course, part and parcel of the
facilitation of communication just mentioned. The leader is willing
to give new ideas a hearing and in many instances effective leaders
are known for their "open-door" policy in encouraging members
to present to them relevant facts and views about situations which
require attention.

RESTRAINT AND PREDICTABILITY

In Chapter 1 we noted the importance of restraint in the use of
power. In effective leadership, this is evidenced by the necessity of
the leader to display a degree of emotional balance in his relationships with others so that he is predictable in performance rather
than being impulsive and given to instability. Particularly important is this in the matter of the distribution of rewards. The leader
has a great deal of visibility and therefore his actions will be interpreted in some sense as signifying the "goodness" or "badness" of
the actions of group members. By rewarding those actions which
are in the interest of the group and judiciously avoiding the rewarding of behaviors which are inimical to the group's best interest, the leader gains respect for his fairness in this function.

A common way of referring to the matter of predictability or dependability is to ask where a person "stands" as well as what he "stands for." In any social relationship, regularities of behavior are valued for the ease with which they may be anticipated. The leader who takes a "stand" which serves as a continuing guide to his responses is more likely to maintain his position, other things equal, than he would with a characteristic tendency toward vacillation of action. This is not to be interpreted, however, as support for a maladaptive rigidity of stance.

ADVOCACY

The function of representation, mentioned earlier in connection with the organizational leader in Chapter 3, may be thought of as involving advocacy. By this we refer to the leader's ability to communicate to other groups and to higher authority the particular desires and needs of his group in order to facilitate its achievement of goals, as is noted by Pelz (1952). Granting that there may be an implicit conflict between the groups within an organizational structure, it is the effective leader who stands as the primary spokesman for his group's interest in such dealings. In some important ways, his functioning in that role has certain consequences to his ability to bring about a degree of goal orientation and goal attainment within his own group. Where he is seen to be loyal to the group's goals, and to be functioning in terms of the group's best interests, as against his own self-interest, the prospect is increased that he will be successful in his influence attempts within the group.

Implications for influence process

This enumeration of some of the characteristics associated with leader effectiveness provides us with a basis for considering how these may have generality for broader processes of influence. The essential point with which we have been concerned relates to behaviors which evoke from followers a positive response. And we take this concern to have a bearing upon other kinds of social influence relationships in terms of their having a fundamental integrity in a *general* process. Thus, while research on leadership, conformity, mass communication, and attitude change is largely fractionated, all involve a transaction, often of a reciprocal variety, between persons or groups in a co-acting relationship.

Indeed, a key approach to social psychology today rests in an understanding of three general elements which appear to be part of all of the influence relationships noted. These elements may be characterized variously but resolve down to: 1) an influence source (or agent or group or communicator) with attributes perceived from actual or implied interactions; 2) some mode of interpersonal activity or other communication; and 3) a recipient (or follower or audience) with personal motivations, perceptions, and reference group affiliations. Whatever their particular designation, all three of these elements are involved in influence process; moreover, sufficient guidelines exist from the work done under apparently diverse headings to develop a coalescence of theory using terms at a common level of abstraction.

From our considerations here, it is evident that leadership especially has produced a study of the influence process as a transaction or interplay between characteristics of the influence agent and those of respondents within a particular social structure. But a parallel development may be found in the work on attitude change. By a rather simple translation it is possible to see the leader as a communication source and to see his behaviors or attributes as communications given off to an audience of recipients within a given social situation. Rather than being passive receptacles for these communications, it would appear now that a selective processing by the recipient goes on. With reference to attitude change, for example, this point has recently been elaborated by Bauer (1964). And, though studies of conformity appear at first glance to be of a different order, they usually involve these elements as well. The difficulty in seeing this arises in part from the essentially nonfunctional groups that are contrived in many of the traditional studies of sources of conformity. Where interaction is thus limited, correspondingly little concern exists for the interplay of relationships, or for the relevance of the conforming response to a focal group activity. However, the group itself can be seen as an influence source whose characteristics—for example, in terms of attraction to members—become relevant to the acceptance of its influence by recipients.

In sum, within these areas of leadership, attitude change, and conformity, clear parallels can be seen for the operation of these three essential elements. Following through on this integration, it is convenient to employ leadership as an illustration of the general process.

THE INFLUENCE AGENT

Observed attributes and behaviors of the influence agent, or leader, contribute to the perception others hold of him as a communication source. What he seems to be, in the sense for example of his upholding the appropriate reference group, fits the specific condition mentioned above in connection with the attributive expectancy of identification and the behavior of advocacy. How he stands on issues, and whether dependably so or not, lends substance to his acceptance in the sense of his credibility as a source. We may in fact think of credibility as a special case of the competence variable stressed here as an attribute of leadership. Taken together with the impression that the leader identifies with group interests vital to the individual, credibility enhances influence potential. This has implications as well for the individual's conformity response to one or more members of a group where he desires their acceptance.

THE COMMUNICATION

An influence agent's communications can involve all of those things he presents to others, verbally or otherwise. Whether they are called "leaders" or not, influence agents communicate messages and these may be essentially of two kinds, not entirely distinct from one another. First, there may be messages of directed content concerning objects and events, e.g. value-laden statements of an attitudinal sort or "factual" statements, presumed to be less value-laden; second, there are messages in the nature of self-references by the communicator. Goffman (1959) has put the latter well in terms of his concept of "impression management." One parallel here may be seen in connection with techniques of propaganda. The propagandist would be using directed messages when employing the technique of "card-stacking" or "glittering generalities." However, by introducing a "plain-folks" theme within his appeal, he provides a self-reference aimed at placing himself within a favorable range of response by the recipient. In so doing, he wishes to increase his credibility by making known his identification with things valued by the recipient. The key then to response to the influence assertion of a communication rests in how it is processed and understood by the recipient. This takes place in the context of two kinds of need systems, his impelling personal motivations and his salient reference group affiliations, matched against what he, the recipient, has come to know about the source.

THE RECIPIENT OF THE COMMUNICATION

What a communication evokes depends upon the recipient's perception of both the message and the source. This seems as true of direct leader-follower interaction as of propaganda effects, once certain translations are made and a common level of abstraction is attained. Each communication may be conceived as being both assessed within the framework of personal motivations and reference group affiliations of the moment as well as itself instigating for their selective operation. Thus, influence agents seek to and often succeed in playing upon these need systems in their encounters with recipients. In the sense of a change in the recipient, influence is achieved by showing direction for the attainment of goals or by enhancing the desirability of a given reference group affiliation and a degree of compliance with its social expectancies.

Conformity depends especially upon the relation of these need systems under conditions where a reliance on the group is necessary to the achievement of an impelling personal motivation, e.g. for "reality" under conditions of ambiguity. In short, the message from groups as influence agents is frequently one of offering satisfaction of personal needs for the acceptance of group standards. This is an essential exchange represented in the "idiosyncrasy credit" concept.

In conclusion

The view that social interaction constitutes an exchange of rewards is not novel in social psychology (cf. Homans, 1958, 1961; and Thibaut & Kelley, 1959). However, there has been far less inclination to view the leader-follower relationship in these terms. Leader characteristics continue to be a dominant focus of attention and in any discussion of "leader effectiveness" this tendency is all the more enhanced. Quite to the contrary, we have been urging here that an understanding of leader effectiveness cannot disregard how the follower fares in the relationship. This helps to elucidate further the point noted earlier from Fillmore Sanford (1950) that a study of followers can provide important returns as a key to leadership. The essential nub of the matter, then, is that once having attained leadership, its maintenance depends upon not only the instrumental matter of goals, but the nature of member interactions and their outcomes.

We have also sought here to extend the conception of leadership to the wider reaches of more general influence process by pointing to lines of convergence with the study of attitude change and conformity. Let it be noted, however, it is *not* our contention that these are identical phenomena, in some sense of a simple reductionism, but that common elements can be discerned in them all, given certain extrapolations beyond confining terms. The intent is to present leadership as one of a number of phenomena which share in broader influence process.

Within the context of influence process, then, leadership phenomena can be seen as one kind of transaction. Accordingly, leader effectiveness depends upon an equity in social exchange with the leader gaining status and exercising influence while helping the group to achieve desired mutual outcomes as well as such individual social rewards as are illustrated by recognition. Goal attainment by itself therefore is not a sufficient condition for effective leadership. A significant concomitant is the process, the relationship along the way, by which group members are able to fulfill their needs for meaningful social participation.

Bibliography

Adorno, T. W., Frenkel-Brunswik, Else, Levinson, D. J., & Sanford, R. N. *The authoritarian personality.* New York: Harper, 1950.

Anderhalter, O. F., Wilkins, W. L., & Rigby, Marilyn K. Peer ratings. *Tech. Rep. No. 2.* St. Louis: St. Louis Univer., 1952.

Arensberg, C. M., & McGregor, D. Determination of morale in an industrial company. *Appl. Anthrop.,* 1942, 1, 12-34.

Asch, S. E. Forming impressions of personality. *J. abnorm. soc. Psychol.,* 1946, 41, 258-290.

Asch, S. E. Effects of group pressure upon the modification and distortion of judgment. In H. Guetzkow (Ed.), *Groups, leadership and men.* Pittsburgh: Carnegie Press, 1951.

Asch, S. E. Studies of independence and conformity: A minority of one against a unanimous majority. *Psychol. Monogr.,* 1956, 70, No. 9 (Whole No. 416).

Bair, J. T. Non-test predictors of attrition in the Naval Air Training Program. *Project No. NM 001 058.05.02.* Pensacola, Florida: U.S. Naval School of Aviation Medicine, 28 April 1952.

Bair, J. T., & Hollander, E. P. Studies in motivation of student aviators at the Naval School of Aviation Medicine. *J. aviat. Med.,* 1953, 24, 514-517, 522.

Bales, R. F., & Slater, P. E. Role differentiation in small decision-making groups. In T. Parsons, R. F. Bales, *et al.* (Eds.), *Family, socialization, and interaction process.* Glencoe, Ill.: Free Press, 1955.

Bass, B. M., McGehee, C. R., Hawkins, W. C., Young, P. C., & Gebel, A. S. Personality variables related to leaderless group discussion behavior. *J. abnorm. soc. Psychol.,* 1953, 48, 120-128.

Bates, F. L. Position, role and status: A reformulation of concepts. *Soc. Forces,* 1956, 34, 313-321.

239

Bauer, R. A. The obstinate audience: The influence process from the point of view of social communication. *Amer. Psychologist*, 1964, 19, 319-328.

Bavelas, A. Leadership: Man and function. *Admin. Sci. Quart.*, 1960, 4, 491-498.

Bell, G. B., & French, R. L. Consistency of individual leadership position in small groups of varying membership. *J. abnorm. soc. Psychol.*, 1950, 45, 764-767.

Bender, I. E., & Hastorf, A. H. On measuring generalized empathic ability (social sensitivity). *J. abnorm. soc. Psychol.*, 1953, 48, 503-506.

Bernberg, R. E. A measure of social conformity. *J. Psychol.*, 1955, 39, 89-96.

Bovard, E. W. Conformity to social norms and attraction to the group. *Science*, 1953, 118, 598-599.

Brown, J. F. *Psychology and the social order*. New York: McGraw-Hill, 1936.

Bruner, J. S. On perceptual readiness. *Psychol. Rev.*, 1957, 64, 123-152.

Bruner, J. S., Shapiro, D., & Tagiuri, R. The meaning of traits in isolation and in combination. In R. Tagiuri & L. Petrullo (Eds.), *Person perception and interpersonal behavior*. Stanford, Calif.: Stanford Univer. Press, 1958. Pp. 277-288.

Cantor, N. F. *Learning through discussion*. Buffalo, N.Y.: Human Relations for Industry, 1951.

Cantril, H. *The psychology of social movements*. New York: Wiley, 1941.

Carter, L. F. Recording and evaluating the performance of individuals as members of small groups. *Personnel Psychol.*, 1954, 7, 477-484.

Carter, L. F., Haythorn, W., Meirowitz, B., & Lanzetta, J. The relation of categorizations and ratings in the observation of group behavior. *Hum. Relat.*, 1951, 4, 239-253.

Carter, L. F., Haythorn, W., Shriver, Beatrice, & Lanzetta, J. The behavior of leaders and other group members. *J. abnorm. soc. Psychol.*, 1951, 46, 589-595.

Cartwright, D. Some principles of mass persuasion: Selected findings of research on the sale of United States war bonds. *Hum. Relat.*, 1949, 2, 253-267.

Cartwright, D. Achieving change in people: Some applications of group dynamics theory. *Hum. Relat.*, 1951, 4, 381-393.

Cartwright, D., & Zander, A. (Eds.) *Group dynamics*. Evanston, Ill.: Row, Peterson, 1960.

Chowdhry, Kamla, & Newcomb, T. M. The relative abilities of leaders and non-leaders to estimate opinions of their own groups. *J. abnorm. soc. Psychol.*, 1952, 47, 51-57.

Christie, R. Changes in authoritarianism as related to situational factors. *Amer. Psychologist*, 1952, 7, 307. (Abstract)

Coch, L., & French, J. R. P., Jr. Overcoming resistance to change. *Hum. Relat.*, 1948, 1, 512-532.

Cowley, W. H. The traits of face-to-face leaders. *J. abnorm. soc. Psychol.*, 1931, 26, 304-313.

Crannell, C. W., & Mollenkopf, W. G. Combat leadership. Chapter III in *AAF Aviation Psychology Program, Research Report No. 14*. Washington, D.C.: U.S. Government Printing Office, 1947.

Criswell, Joan H. Sociometric methods of measuring group preferences. *Sociometry*, 1943, 6, 398-408.

Criswell, Joan H. Foundations of sociometric measurement. *Sociometry*, 1946, 9, 7-14.

Criswell, Joan H. Sociometric concepts in personnel administration. *Sociometry*, 1949, 12, 287-300.

Cronbach, L. J. Proposals leading to the analytic treatment of social perception scores. In R. Tagiuri & L. Petrullo (Eds.), *Person perception and interpersonal behavior*. Stanford, Calif.: Stanford Univer. Press, 1958.

Cronbach, L. J., & Gleser, Goldine, C. Assessing similarity between profiles. *Psychol. Bull.*, 1953, 50, 456-474.

Crutchfield, R. S. Conformity and character. *Amer. Psychologist*, 1955, 10, 191-198.

David, H. P., & Brengelmann, J. C. (Eds.) *Perspectives in personality research*. New York: Springer Publishing Co., 1960.

Deutsch, M., & Gerard, H. B. A study of normative and informational social influences upon individual judgment. *J. abnorm. soc. Psychol.*, 1955, 51, 629-636.

Dittes, J. E., & Kelley, H. H. Effects of different conditions of acceptance upon conformity to group norms. *J. abnorm. soc. Psychol.*, 1956, 53, 100-107.

Duncan, D. B. Multiple range and multiple F tests. *Biometrics*, 1955, 11, 1-42.

Edwards, A. L. *Experimental design in psychological research*. (Rev. ed.) New York: Rinehart, 1960.

Festinger, L. Informal social communication. *Psychol. Rev.*, 1950, 57, 271-282.

Fiedler, F. E. Assumed similarity measures as predictors of team effectiveness. *J. abnorm. soc. Psychol.*, 1954, 49, 381-388.

Flanagan, J. C. *AAF Aviation Psychology Program, Research Report No. 1*, Washington, D.C.: U.S. Government Printing Office, 1948.

Flyer, E. S., Barron, E., & Bigbee, L. Discrepancies between self-descriptions and group ratings as measures of lack of insight. *Res. Bull.* 53-33. San Antonio, Texas: Human Resources Research Center, Lackland Air Force Base, 1953.

French, J. R. P., Jr., & Zander, A. The group dynamics approach. *Psychol. Labor-Management Relat.*, 1949, 71-80.

Gardner, E. F., & Thompson, G. C. *Social relations and morale in small groups*. New York: Appleton, 1956.

Gibb, C. A. The principles and traits of leadership. *J. abnorm. soc. Psychol.*, 1947, 42, 267-284.

Gibb, C. A. The sociometry of leadership in temporary groups. *Sociometry*, 1950, 13, 226-243.

Gibb, C. A. Leadership. In G. Lindzey (Ed.), *Handbook of social psychology.* Vol. II. Cambridge, Mass.: Addison-Wesley, 1954.

Goffman, E. *The presentation of self in everyday life.* Garden City, N.Y.: Doubleday Anchor, 1959.

Gouldner, A. W. (Ed.) *Studies in leadership.* New York: Harper, 1950.

Guetzkow, H. (Ed.) *Groups, leadership and men.* Pittsburgh: Carnegie Press, 1951.

Havron, D., Fay, R., & Goodacre, D. *The effectiveness of small military units.* Washington, D.C.: Institute for Research in Human Relations, 1951.

Heider, F. *The psychology of interpersonal relations.* New York: Wiley, 1958.

Hemphill, J. K. *Situational factors in leadership.* Columbus: Ohio State Univer., 1949.

Hemphill, J. K. Administration as problem-solving. In A. W. Halpin (Ed.), *Administrative theory in education.* Chicago: Midwest Administration Center, 1958.

Hemphill, J. K. Why people attempt to lead. In L. Petrullo & B. M. Bass (Eds.), *Leadership and interpersonal behavior.* New York: Holt, Rinehart, & Winston, 1961.

Herzberg, F., Mausner, B., & Snyderman, Barbara. *The motivation to work.* New York: Wiley, 1959.

Hollander, E. P. An investigation of the relationship between academic performance in pre-flight and success or failure in basic flight training. *Project No. NM 001 058.17.01.* Pensacola, Florida: U.S. Naval School of Aviation Medicine, 24 November 1952.

Hollander, E. P. Authoritarianism and leadership choice in a military setting. *J. abnorm. soc. Psychol.,* 1954, 49, 365-370. (a)

Hollander, E. P. Buddy ratings: Military research and industrial implications. *Personnel Psychol.,* 1954, 7, 385-393. (b)

Hollander, E. P. Peer nominations on leadership as a predictor of the pass-fail criterion in Naval Air Training. *J. appl. Psychol.,* 1954, 38, 150-153. (c)

Hollander, E. P. Studies of leadership among naval aviation cadets. *J. aviat. Med.,* 1954, 25, 164-170, 200. (d)

Hollander, E. P. Conditions affecting the military utilization of peer ratings: The Newport study. I. Reliability. *Navy Tech. Rep. 1-56.* Pittsburgh: Psychological Laboratories, Carnegie Institute of Technology, January 1956. (a)

Hollander, E. P. Conditions affecting the military utilization of peer ratings: The Newport study. II. Validity against in-training criteria. *Navy Tech. Rep. 2-56.* Pittsburgh: Psychological Laboratories, Carnegie Institute of Technology, February 1956. (b)

Hollander, E. P. Conditions affecting the military utilization of peer ratings: The Newport study. III. Friendship choice. *Navy Tech. Rep. 3-56.* Pittsburgh: Psychological Laboratories, Carnegie Institute of Technology, April 1956. (c)

Hollander, E. P. Conditions affecting the military utilization of peer ratings: The Newport study. *Final report.* ONR Contract 760(06). Pittsburgh: Psychological Laboratories, Carnegie Institute of Technology, May 1956. (d)

Hollander, E. P. A better military rating system through peer ratings. ONR *Res. Rev.*, July 1956, 16-20. (e)

Hollander, E. P. The friendship factor in peer nominations. *Personnel Psychol.*, 1956, 9, 435-447. (f)

Hollander, E. P. Interpersonal exposure time as a determinant of the predictive utility of peer ratings. *Psychol. Reps.*, 1956, 2, 445-448. (g)

Hollander, E. P. The reliability of peer nominations under various conditions of administration. *J. appl. Psychol.*, 1957, 41, 2, 85-90.

Hollander, E. P. Conformity, status, and idiosyncrasy credit. *Psychol. Rev.*, 1958, 65, 117-127. (a)

Hollander, E. P. Some further findings on leadership, followership, and friendship. ONR *Tech. Rep. IV.* Pittsburgh: Carnegie Institute of Technology, Nov. 1958. (b)

Hollander, E. P. Group consensus and group attraction. ONR *Tech. Rep. No. VI.* Pittsburgh: Carnegie Institute of Technology, April 1959. (a)

Hollander, E. P. Some points of reinterpretation regarding social conformity. *Sociol. Rev.* (England), 1959, 7, 159-168 (b).

Hollander, E. P. Competence and conformity in the acceptance of influence. *J. abnorm. soc. Psychol.*, 1960, 61, 365-369. (a)

Hollander, E. P. On the issue of conformity in personality. In H. P. David & J. C. Brengelmann (Eds.), *Perspectives in personality research.* New York: Springer, 1960. (b)

Hollander, E. P. Emergent leadership and social influence. In L. Petrullo & B. M. Bass (Eds.), *Leadership and interpersonal behavior.* New York: Holt, Rinehart, & Winston, 1961. Pp. 30-47. (a)

Hollander, E. P. Some effects of perceived status on responses to innovative behavior. *J. abnorm. soc. Psychol.*, 1961, 63, 247-250. (b)

Hollander, E. P., & Bair, J. T. Attitudes toward authority-figures as correlates of motivation among naval aviation cadets. *J. appl. Psychol.*, 1954, 38, 1, 21-25.

Hollander, E. P., & Webb, W. B. Leadership, followership, and friendship: An analysis of peer nominations. *J. abnorm. soc. Psychol.*, 1955, 50, 163-167.

Hollander, E. P., & Willis, R. H. Conformity, independence and anticonformity as determiners of perceived influence and attraction. Paper read at Eastern Psychological Association, Philadelphia, Pa., April 1964.

Homans, G. C. *The human group.* New York: Harcourt, Brace, 1950.

Homans, G. C. Social behavior as exchange. *Amer. J. Sociol.*, 1958, 63, 597-606.

Homans, G. C. *Social behavior: Its elementary forms.* New York: Harcourt, Brace, 1961.

Hyman, H. H. The psychology of status. *Arch. Psychol.*, 1942, No. 269.

Institute for Research in Human Relations. *Leadership identification and acceptance.* Philadelphia: The Institute, February 1952.

Jackson, J. M., & Saltzstein, H. D. *Group membership and conformity processes.* Ann Arbor, Mich.: Research Center for Group Dynamics, 1956.

Jackson, J. M., & Saltzstein, H. D. The effect of person-group relationships on conformity processes. *J. abnorm. soc. Psychol.*, 1958, 57, 17-24.

Jacobson, E. H. Foreman-steward participation practices and worker attitudes in a unionized factory. Unpublished doctoral dissertation, Univer. of Michigan, 1951.

Jahoda, Marie. Conformity and independence: A psychological analysis. *Hum. Relat.*, 1959, 12, 99-120.

Jenkins, J. G. The nominating technique as a method of evaluating air group morale. *J. aviat. Med.*, 1948, 19, 12-19.

Jenkins, W. O. A review of leadership studies with particular reference to military problems. *Psychol. Bull.*, 1947, 44, 54-79.

Jennings, Helen H. *Leadership and isolation.* New York: Longmans, Green, 1943 (Rev. ed., 1950).

Jennings, Helen H. Sociometry of leadership. *Sociometry Monogr.*, 1947, 14, 12-24.

Jones, E. E., & deCharms, R. Changes in social perception as a function of the personal relevance of behavior. *Sociometry*, 1957, 20, 75-85.

Julian, J. W., & Steiner, I. D. Perceived acceptance as a determinant of conformity behavior. *J. soc. Psychol.*, 1961, 55, 191-198.

Kahn, R. L., & Katz, D. Leadership practices in relation to productivity and morale. In D. Cartwright & A. Zander (Eds.), *Group dynamics: Research and theory.* Evanston, Ill.: Row, Peterson, 1953.

Katz, D. Employee groups: What motivates them and how they perform. *Advanc. Mgmt.*, 1949, 14, 119-124. (a)

Katz, D. Morale and motivation in industry. In W. Dennis (Ed.), *Current trends in industrial psychology.* Pittsburgh: Univer. of Pittsburgh Press, 1949. Pp. 145-171. (b)

Katz, D., Maccoby, N., & Morse, N. C. *Productivity, supervision and morale in an office situation.* Survey Research Center, Univer. of Michigan, 1950.

Katz, D., Maccoby, N., Gurin, G., & Floor, L. G. *Productivity, supervision and morale among railroad workers.* Survey Research Center, Univer. of Michigan, 1951.

Katz, E., & Lazarsfeld, P. F. *Personal influence.* Glencoe, Ill.: Free Press, 1955.

Katz, L. A new status index derived from sociometric analysis. *Psychometrika*, 1953, 18, 39-43.

Krech, D. Psychological theory and social psychology. In H. Helson (Ed.), *Theoretical foundations of psychology.* New York: D. Van Nostrand, 1951.

Kubany, A. J. Evaluation of medical student clinical performance: A criterion study. Unpublished doctoral dissertation, Univer. of Pittsburgh, 1957.

Lawrence, P. R. How to deal with resistance to change. *Harvard Bus. Rev.*, 1954, 32, 49-57.

Lemann, T. B., & Solomon, R. L. Group characteristics as revealed in sociometric patterns and personality ratings. *Sociometry*, 1952, 15, 7-90.

Lewin, K. Group decision and social change. In T. M. Newcomb & E. L. Hartley (Eds.), *Readings in social psychology*. New York: Henry Holt & Co., 1947. Pp. 330-344.

Lewin, K., Lippitt, R., & White, R. K. Patterns of aggressive behavior in experimentally created "social climates." *J. soc. Psychol.*, 1939, 10, 271-299.

Likert, R. Motivation and productivity. *Mgmt. Rec.*, 1956, 18, 128-131.

Likert, R. *New patterns of management*. New York: McGraw-Hill, 1961.

McClelland, D. C. Personality. In P. R. Farnsworth (Ed.), *Annual review of psychology*. Palo Alto, Cal.: Annual Reviews, Inc., 1956.

McClure, G. E., Tupes, E. C., & Dailey, J. T. Research on criteria of officer effectiveness. *USAF Hum. Resour. Res. Cent., Res. Bull. No. 51-8*, 1951.

McGregor, D. Conditions of effective leadership in industrial organization. *J. consult. Psychol.*, 1944, 8, 56-63.

March, J. G. Group norms and the active minority. *Amer. sociol. Rev.*, 1954, 19, 733-741.

Marrow, A. J. *Making management human*. New York: McGraw-Hill, 1957.

Marrow, A. J., & French, J. R. P., Jr. Changing a stereotype in industry. *J. soc. Issues*, 1945, 1, 33-37.

Maslow, A. H. The authoritarian character structure. *J. soc. Psychol.*, 1943, 18, 401-411.

Matthews, J. Research on the development of valid situational tests of leadership: 1. Survey of the literature. *Personnel Research Section, Rep. No. 912*, Washington, D.C.: Department of the Army, Oct. 1951.

Mead, G. H. *Mind, self, and society*. Chicago: Univer. of Chicago Press, 1934.

Menzel, H., & Katz, E. Social relations and innovations in the medical profession: The epidemiology of a new drug. *Publ. Opin. Quart.*, 1955, 19, 337-352.

Miller, N. A., & Dollard, J. *Social learning and imitation*. New Haven: Yale Univer. Press, 1941.

Moore, O. K., & Berkowitz, M. I. Problem solving and social interaction. *ONR Tech. Rep. No. 1*. Contract Nonr-609(16). New Haven: Yale Univer., Dept. of Sociol., 1956.

Moreno, J. L. *Who shall survive?* New York: Beacon House, 1934 (Rev. ed., 1953).

Newcomb, T. M. *Social psychology*. New York: Holt, Rinehart & Winston, 1950.

Newcomb, T. M. The prediction of interpersonal attraction. *Amer. Psychologist*, 1956, 11, 575-586.

Newcomb, T. M. *The acquaintance process*. New York: Holt, Rinehart, & Winston, 1961.

Northway, M. L. A method for depicting social relationships obtained by sociometric testing. *Sociometry*, 1940, 3, 144-150.

Osgood, C. E., & Tannenbaum, P. H. The principle of congruity in the prediction of attitude change. *Psychol. Rev.*, 1955, 62, 42-55.

Peatman, J. G. *Descriptive and sampling statistics.* New York: Harper, 1947.

Pelz, D. C. Influence: A key to effective leadership in the first-line supervisor. *Personnel*, 1952, 29, 209-217.

Pepinsky, Pauline. Social exceptions that prove the rule. In B. M. Bass & I. A. Berg (Eds.), *Conformity and deviation.* New York: Harper, 1961.

Pepinsky, Pauline, Hemphill, J. K., & Shevitz, R. N. Attempts to lead, group productivity, and morale under conditions of acceptance and rejection. *J. abnorm. soc. Psychol.*, 1958, 57, 47-54.

Pepitone, A. Attributions of causality, social attitudes, and cognitive matching processes. In R. Tagiuri & L. Petrullo (Eds.), *Person perception and interpersonal behavior.* Stanford, Calif.: Stanford Univer. Press, 1958. Pp. 258-276.

Petrullo, L., & Bass, B. M. (Eds.). *Leadership and interpersonal behavior.* New York: Holt, Rinehart & Winston, 1961.

Postman, L., Bruner, J. S., & McGinnies, E. Personal values as selective factors in perception. *J. abnorm. soc. Psychol.*, 1948, 43, 142-154.

Proctor, C. H., & Loomis, C. P. Analysis of sociometric data. In Marie Jahoda, *et al.* (Eds.), *Research methods in social relations* (Part 2). New York: Dryden Press, 1951. Pp. 561-585.

Purcell, T. V. *Blue collar man.* Cambridge, Mass.: Harvard Univer. Press, 1960.

Ricciuti, H. N., & French, J. W. Development of personality tests for naval officer selection: I. Analysis of U.S. Naval Academy criterion of aptitude for service. *Tech. Rep. No. 1.* Princeton, N. J.: Educational Testing Service, March 1951.

Richardson, Bellows, Henry & Co. A report evaluating leadership potential of pre-flight navcads. ONR *Contract Nonr 0-3400* (RBH Project 203), 1951.

Riecken, H. W. The effect of talkativeness on ability to influence group solutions to problems. *Sociometry*, 1958, 21, 309-321.

Rohde, K. J. The relation of authoritarianism of the air crew member to his acceptance by the airplane commander. *Amer. Psychologist*, 1951, 6, 323. (Abstract)

Rokeach, M. Generalized mental rigidity as a factor in ethnocentrism. *J. abnorm. soc. Psychol.*, 1948, 43, 259-278.

Saenger, G., & Proshansky, H. Projective techniques in the service of attitude research. *Personality*, 1950, 2, 23-24.

Sanford, F. H. *Authoritarianism and leadership.* Philadelphia: Institute for Research in Human Relations, 1950.

Sanford, N. Surface and depth in the individual personality. *Psychol. Rev.*, 1956, 63, 349-359.

Schachter, S. Deviation, rejection, and communication. *J. abnorm. soc. Psychol.,* 1951, 46, 190-207.

Schein, E. H. The effect of reward on adult imitative behavior. *J. abnorm. soc. Psychol.,* 1954, 49, 389-395.

Schwab, R. E. Participative management—The solution to the human relations problem? Address given before the Cincinnati Chapter of the Society for the Advancement of Management, October 2, 1952.

Scodel, A., & Mussen, P. Social perceptions of authoritarians and nonauthoritarians. *J. abnorm. soc. Psychol.,* 1953, 48, 181-184.

Sears, R. R. A theoretical framework for personality and social behavior. *Amer. Psychologist,* 1951, 6, 476-484.

Seashore, S. E. *Group cohesiveness in the industrial work group.* Ann Arbor: Univer. of Michigan Press, 1954.

Sherif, M. *An outline of social psychology.* New York: Harper, 1948.

Smith, R. G., & Westen, R. J. Studies of morale methodology and criteria. *USAF Hum. Resources Res. Center, Res. Bull. No. 51-29,* 1951.

Steiner, I. D. Interpersonal behavior as influenced by accuracy of social perception. *Psychol. Rev.,* 1955, 62, 268-274.

Stogdill, R. M. Personal factors associated with leadership: A survey of the literature. *J. Psychol.,* 1948, 25, 37-51.

Stogdill, R. M., *et al.* Studies in naval leadership: The prediction of naval officer performance. *ONR Contract N6ori-17.* Columbus: The Ohio State Research Foundation, 1953.

Stouffer, S. A., *et al. The American soldier.* Princeton: Princeton Univer. Press, 1949. 2 vols.

Suci, G. J., Vallance, T. R., & Glickman, A. S. An analysis of peer ratings: 1. The assessment of reliability of several question forms and techniques used at the Naval Officer Candidate School. *Tech. Bull. 54-9.* Washington, D.C.: Bureau of Naval Personnel, June 1954.

Tagiuri, R. Relational analysis: An extension of sociometric method with emphasis upon social perception. *Sociometry,* 1952, 15, 91-104.

Tagiuri, R., & Petrullo, L. (Eds.). *Person perception and interpersonal behavior.* Stanford, Calif.: Stanford Univer. Press, 1958.

Talland, G. A. The assessment of group opinion by leaders, and their influence on its formation. *J. abnorm. soc. Psychol.,* 1954, 49, 431-434.

Thibaut, J. W., & Kelley, H. H. *The social psychology of groups.* New York: Wiley, 1959.

Thibaut, J. W., & Riecken, H. W. Some determinants and consequences of the perception of social causality. *J. Pers.,* 1955, 24, 113-133.

Thibaut, J. W., & Strickland, L. H. Psychological set and social conformity. *J. Pers.,* 1956, 25, 115-129.

Thomas, W. I. A theory of social personality. In E. H. Volkart (Ed.), *Social behavior and personality.* New York: Soc. Sci. Res. Council, 1951.

Titus, H. E., & Hollander, E. P. The California F Scale in psychological research: 1950-55. *Psychol. Bull.,* 1957, 54, 47-64.

Trist, E. L., & Bamforth, K. W. Some social psychological consequences of the long-wall method of coal-getting. *Hum. Relat.*, 1951, 4, 3-38.

Tupes, E. C., Borg, W. R., & Friedman, G. A factor analysis of the OCS paired-comparison evaluation system. *USAF Hum. Resources Res. Cent., Tech. Rep. No. 53-10.*, 1953.

van Zelst, R. H. Worker popularity and job satisfaction. *Personnel Psychol.*, 1951, 4, 405-412.

van Zelst, R. H. Sociometrically selected work teams increase production. *Personnel Psychol.*, 1952, 5, 175-185.

Vaughn, C. L. The nominating technique. In *New methods in applied psychology.* College Park, Maryland: Univer. of Maryland, 1947. Pp. 22-25.

Viteles, M. S. *Motivation and morale in industry.* New York: Norton, 1953.

Walker, J., & Marriott, R. A study of some attitudes to factory work. *Occup. Psychol.*, 1951, 25, 181-191.

Webb, W. B., & Hollander, E. P. Comparison of three morale measures: A survey, pooled group judgments, and self evaluation. *J. appl. Psychol.*, 1956, 40, 17-20.

Wherry, R. J., & Fryer, D. H. Buddy ratings: Popularity contest or leadership criterion? *Personnel Psychol.*, 1949, 2, 147-159.

Williams, S. B., & Leavitt, H. J. Group opinion as a predictor of military leadership. *J. consult. Psychol.*, 1947, 11, 283-291.

Willis, R. H. Two dimensions of conformity-nonconformity. *Sociometry*, 1963, 26, 499-513.

Willis, R. H. Conformity, independence, and anticonformity. *Hum. Relat.*, in press.

Willis, R. H., & Hollander, E. P. An experimental study of three response modes in social influence situations. *J. abnorm. soc. Psychol.*, 1964, in press.

———

Personnel Research Section, AGO, *Rep.* #767. Follow-up study of officer performance of West Point graduates. Washington, D.C., 1948.

Personnel Research Section, AGO, *Rep.* #811. Follow-up validation of predictor instruments for West Point classes of 1944, 1945, and 1946 against 1948 ratings on DA AGO Form 67-1. Washington, D.C., 1949.

Name index

Adorno, T. W., 45, 52, 165, 191, 239
Anderhalter, O. F., 94, 98, 112, 239
Arensberg, C. M., 34, 239
Asch, S. E., 183, 184, 206, 214, 239

Bair, J. T., 57-65, 61, 63, 141, 239, 243
Bales, R. F., 22, 194, 239
Bamforth, K. W., 36, 248
Barron, E., 241
Bass, B. M., 16, 45, 52, 53, 239, 242, 243, 246
Bates, F. L., 154, 164, 239
Bauer, R. A., 234, 240
Bavelas, A., 7, 240
Bell, G. B., 19, 240
Bender, I. E., 165, 191, 240
Berg, I. A., 246
Berkowitz, M. I., 245
Bernberg, R. E., 184, 240
Bigbee, L., 241
Borg, W. R., 93, 248
Bovard, E. W., 166, 189, 240
Boyle, R., 181
Brengelmann, J. C., 179, 241, 243

Brown, J. F., 26, 240
Bruner, J. S., 164, 206, 240, **246**

Cantor, N. F., 40, 240
Cantril, H., 57, 240
Carter, L. F., 19, 52, 53, 194, 240
Cartwright, D., 5, 12, 231, 240, 244
Chowdhry, Kamla, 170, 175, 240
Christie, R., 45, 51, 240
Coch, L., 37, 240
Cowley, W. H., 18, 241
Crannell, C. W., 54, 241
Criswell, Joan H., 22, 67, 89, 241
Cronbach, L. J., 77, 79, 241
Crutchfield, R. S., 183, 184, 241

Dailey, J. T., 100, 245
Dalton, J., 181
David, H. P., 179, 241, 243
deCharms, R., 20, 172, 177, **244**
Dennis, W., 244
Deutsch, M., 166, 241
Dittes, J. E., 20, 155, 161, 167, 177, 241
Dollard, J., 153, 245
Duncan, D. B., 221, 223, 241

Subject index

253

256   SUBJECT INDEX